A young mother struggles to care for her special-needs child in this debut Christian memoir."

"… Guinn is a skilled dramatist of her own character, unafraid to portray herself in a bad or selfish light. She also writes with a novelistic attention to detail; here, she describes her office at the Cessna factory: "The room smelled of typewriter ribbon, fresh paper, and cigarette smoke that hovered around the ashtray on my desk. The office sounded of tapping on typewriter keys, clicking on adding machines, and an occasional bing on the window next to me when some guy on the assembly line below threw a rivet at the window beside my desk." The result is a substantial and nuanced chronicle of perseverance."

"A rich, complicated account of surviving life's trials."

—*Kirkus Reviews*

♦ ♦ ♦

"In *For the Love of God* by Jackie Guinn, the author utilized suspense to great effect, which made me look forward to subsequent chapters as she filled me in on various events of her life. The book also took me on a roller-coaster of emotions as I read about the unconditional love that Jackie had for Jenny, despite the circumstances of her birth. This thought-provoking work also got me thinking about medical ethics when, at one time, the doctors seemed unwilling to provide the necessary care for Jenny. Jackie also ensures every event and emotion is vividly described, which will help capture the imagination of the reader. Readers will also appreciate the steady narration, which adds to the overall appeal of this memoir. I look forward to reading something else by this author."

—Frank Mutuma, *Readers' Favorite*

✦ ✦ ✦

"*For the Love of God* is a deeply moving and poignant read that captures the essence of parental devotion and the capacity for personal growth and healing. Jackie Guinn's ability to convey emotional depth and impart life lessons in a well-written narrative is commendable. The vivid descriptions of the 70s era add a nostalgic touch and make the book engaging for readers. The social prejudices and challenges of that era give readers a clear picture and better understanding of the complex societal landscape that influenced Jackie's decisions and actions. The contrast between Jackie's grief and loss with her naive introduction to Christianity allows readers to empathize with her and find moments of lightness in her story. The pictures at the end of the book gave it a personal touch that beautifully resonated with the emotions and experiences shared throughout. This is a memorable and heartfelt read. I thoroughly enjoyed this book and highly recommend it to anyone who loves emotionally engaging memoirs."

—Luwi Nyakansaila, *Readers' Favorite*

✦ ✦ ✦

"Author Jackie Guinn gives everything of herself on the page to offer readers a deeply moving memoir that is sure to touch many hearts. Jackie's resilience and unwavering devotion to her daughter are truly inspiring, highlighting the strength that can be found in the face of adversity. I really enjoyed the feel of the narrative, with warm touches and gentle turns of phrase that make it feel as though a dear friend is telling you their story and connecting you to it deeply. Her journey of faith and self-discovery resonated with me on a profound level, reminding me of the power of love and perseverance in the darkest of times. Guinn's honest and heartfelt prose captures the raw emotions of her experiences, inviting readers into her world with empathy and authenticity. I loved the way she described other people who had come into her life for the better. Overall, I would certainly recommend For the Love of God for fans of inspirational true stories everywhere."

—K.C. Finn, *Readers' Favorite*

# FOR THE LOVE OF GOD

## A MEMOIR

### JACKIE GUINN

Merciful Master
BOOKS

MERCIFUL MASTER BOOKS

*For the Love of God: A Memoir*
Copyright © 2024 by Jacquelyn S. Guinn

ISBN – 979-8-9906321-2-7 (hardback)
ISBN – 979-8-218-40570-0 (paperback)
ISBN – 979-8-218-41592-1 (ebook)
ISBN – 979-8-9906321-3-4 (audiobook)

Cover design by Hannah Linder (*hannahlinderdesigns.com*)
Interior design and typesetting by Enterline Design Services (*enterlinedesign.com*)

Printed in the United States of America

2024—First Edition
10 9 8 7 6 5 4 3 2 1

Visit *www.jackieguinn.com*

Disclaimer: The events in this book took place fifty years ago and reflect my recollections of my experiences. While important elements of dialogue and scenes have not been changed, I have had to recreate and/or supplement dialogue and scenes to make them consistent with the event and the character of the person speaking. Some of the names have been changed along with identifying details to protect individual privacy. A few of the events have been compressed.

## THIS BOOK IS DEDICATED TO MY CHILDREN:

Kendra, Jeremiah, Renata, and Micah

I am so thankful that God has shown His great love toward me
through the birth and life of each one of you.

# CHAPTER ONE

I was twenty-two and single when I missed two periods and took a jar of urine to the local clinic. It was the fall of 1971. My heart pounded as the gray-haired woman wrote my name on a sticky label and smashed it on the glass jar.

"You'll get the results in a couple of days," she said without looking up from her paperwork.

After work a few days later, I called for the results.

"Let's see—oh yes—the results are positive." Silence.

A wide grin spread across my face, and my pulse quickened. "Thanks!"

I strolled out of the tall, glass-walled insurance tower and stepped into the windy September heat. I drove my silver Plymouth Duster across the bridge that overlooked the Missouri River to my apartment in North Kansas City. I had to be careful who I told about this, and I sure couldn't tell anyone at work.

I pushed my key through the lock on the front door of my apartment and threw the keys on the yellowish Formica countertop that acted as a barrier between the kitchenette and the rest of the studio apartment. I pulled open the refrigerator door, grabbed a cold bottle of Coke, and traipsed across burnt orange shag carpet that smelled of musk and smoke. After I twisted the knob on the window air conditioner, cool air made its way through the stuffy apartment. My double bed was situated in the center of the room with the headboard against the back wall. After I planted myself on the edge of the bed, I opened a pack of cigarettes and steeled myself for the conversation I was about to have. My fingers shook as I lit a cigarette and placed it in the mustard-colored ceramic ashtray that sat on the end table beside my bed. I took a deep breath, lifted the receiver from the avocado-green desk phone, and dialed my mother, who now lived in Virginia. The phone rang three times before she answered. When Mom realized it was me, she lowered her voice.

"Hi, Jackie," she said and then waited. When I told her the news, she didn't say anything.

"I could move to Virginia, and I would work and pay rent until the baby came." I bit my lower lip and kept wrapping and unwrapping the curled phone cord around my finger.

"You know your dad and I are having problems." After a pause, she added, "We'll probably get a divorce."

I ignored her remark and continued. "After the baby is born, I'll get a babysitter—no—I'll get the babysitter and apartment lined up *before* the baby is born. I won't be any trouble at all—I promise!" It all seemed doable to me, but on the other end, there was a long silence.

"Mom?"

"I'm here," she said. "We have a lot going on right now, and I—I don't think it's a good idea for you to come up here."

"I really would work and pay my way."

Then, Mom broke the silence with the dreaded words, "You could have an abortion."

At the sound of those words, I closed my eyes, and my lips pressed into a grimace. I knew she would say that. "No, I would never do that."

After a polite goodbye, I put the receiver back on the cradle of the desk phone. I took a drink of Coke, crushed my cigarette out in the mustard-colored ashtray, and lay down on the double bed. My apartment was silent except for the humming of the air conditioner.

My stomach turned when I thought about marrying my baby's father, Tony. Too many times I had heard how Tony's brothers' wives called around to bars late at night trying to hunt down their husbands. With Tony's outgoing personality and winning smile, I could see that I would have the same problem, and there was no way in hell I would live like that!

◆ ◆ ◆

In the late 1950s through the mid-70s, there were social rules that everyone understood. Everyone knew that girls didn't call boys, and everyone knew that the boy invited the girl out on a date. He picked her up on Friday night (at the door, of course, because only a schmuck

FOR THE LOVE OF GOD

would sit outside and honk), he paid for the drive-in movie, and he parked in the last row. An hour later, the windows would fog up. In those days, it was possible for girls to get a bad reputation, which was devastating. If a girl got pregnant, she would have to leave school; and if she came back, no one would talk to her. It was also common for parents to forbid their high schoolers to date certain people based on social status. Many successful parents made sure their daughters didn't get too serious with someone from the lower class. Songs like "Patches" by Dicky Lee and "Dawn" by the Four Seasons reflected this social rule.

When teenage girls pulled into a gas station, they cranked down the driver's side window and asked for either regular or ethel. After the cute boy attendant checked the oil, he would try to sneak a peek up a girl's dress as he swiped the squeegee over the windshield.

Daily life was also different. There was more dirt on the ground in those days, so kids had to regularly use a nail scrub brush to clean their fingernails, and since *everyone* washed their hair once a week, they also had to clean the gunk out of their combs.

When kids went to school, boys wore collared shirts that were tucked into their casual pants, and girls wore dresses. Everyone had three sets of clothes: play clothes, school clothes, and Sunday clothes. Of course, not everyone went to church, so Sunday clothes were, really, dress-up clothes—like something a girl would wear when she went downtown to shop.

At home, window air conditioners could only reach the living area, so in order to sleep, people had to push up the window beside their bed and turn on the attic fan. In those days, families ate meals together. No one could start eating until everyone was seated, and kids couldn't leave the table until they said something like "May I be excused, please?"

During that time, there were two means of communication: telephone or letter. Letters would take three days, or two days if they went by airmail, and long-distance phone calls cost money. Thus, when students went away to college, it was unlikely that the high school romance would last. High school graduation meant boys would either go into the service or go to college. Those who went to college learned to protest in the streets and harass those in military uniforms. Those who went into the service learned to march to chants such as "I don't know, but I believe—I'll be home on Christmas Eve." Servicemen followed every oral and written instruction, which included the writing on the inside of the plywood stall: "Flush twice; it's a long way to the chow hall" and "Put on civilian clothes before you get off the plane in the U.S." Similarly, when girls turned eighteen, they would either go to college or get an apartment. *Everyone* had to leave home—sink or swim.

People in those days were raised by parents who were familiar with the effects of the Great Depression; therefore, things like credit cards were not a normal part of people's lives. If people owed money, they didn't sleep until they had figured out a way to pay it back. The government assistance programs that we are familiar with today were not well established and were relatively unknown. People who were physically and/or mentally disabled were sent to state institutions, and homeless people were called hobos.

Until 1962, kids who didn't go to church learned to pray in public schools. Thousands of kids across the United States began the school day with heads bowed and hands folded on top of their desks. I was in Mrs. Hall's sixth-grade class when I learned the Lord's Prayer. After we prayed, our wrinkled, gray-haired teacher bellowed instructions and slammed the ruler on her desk to get our attention. I noticed that people who passed by our classroom as they strolled down the hall would back away when they heard her holler at some boy with a short attention span. On the other hand, those of us *inside* her classroom adored her. Mrs. Hall never scolded us if we asked a question, and she always knew the right way to get information through our thick skulls. All her theatrics didn't bother any of us.

From the sixth grade forward, every night after I turned off the light and pulled the covers over my chest, I closed my eyes and whispered the Lord's Prayer. Who knew what "Our Father who art in heaven, hallowed be thy name" even meant?

# CHAPTER TWO

A few weeks later, I decided to get in touch with my ex-husband. I was having a baby, and I knew I would need help. I had married him when I was nineteen, and by the time I was twenty, I was bored, so I left him. I took a deep breath and picked up the phone. When I told my ex I was pregnant and wanted to talk to him, there was silence and then acceptance.

He was six feet tall, which was a foot taller than I was, and thin. He was clean-cut and raised in a middle-class family with an older sister, who had devastated their parents by getting pregnant at age sixteen.

He picked me up in some car that had replaced his 1963 white Chevy Impala. I remember that he used to dust that car every morning. We drove to a nearby park, and after he turned off the ignition, he continued to stare out the windshield with his hand still on the key. He rolled down the window, lit a cigarette, settled back into the seat, and turned to me. A slight breeze brought in the earthy smells of fall and the sounds of rustling red, yellow, and orange leaves in the trees above us.

"I just—well—I don't really *want* to marry him." My ex didn't say anything but continued to watch me. "I called my mom, and there's no way that's going to happen." I opened the purse on my lap and hunted for a cigarette.

At the thought of us possibly getting back together, his eyes began to sparkle and a half smile formed in the corner of his thin lips.

"If we were to get back together," he said as he rubbed his hands down his pant leg. "I would want you to promise me that the baby will never know that I'm not the father."

We talked for another hour before he dropped me off. I climbed out of the car, but before I closed the door, he said, "Wait a minute." I bent down and gazed at him through the open window on the passenger's side.

"When you decide what you want to do—just—just let me know. Give me a call or something." He cleared his throat and rubbed the back of his neck. I smiled and thanked him for the conversation. Although my ex was receptive, I just didn't have feelings for him, so I never called.

I did, however, have feelings for Tony. A few weeks later, I stood in front of my baby's father with my head lifted and arms crossed. "I'll marry you on one condition." Tony tilted his head and raised his eyebrows. "You have to get a job in another state. I don't care where it is as long as we're away from Kansas City and your brothers." Tony's blue eyes sparkled as he gave me a wide grin.

♦ ♦ ♦

On a cold, dark February evening in 1972, I wore a brown maternity dress as I stood beside Tony in front of a justice of the peace. My sister, Vicki, was next to me, and Tony's younger brother stood next to him. It was about 7:00 p.m. when we all faced the balding, older man. A couple of lamps provided a warm glow to the dark-paneled room. The chamber contained a heavy desk and tall, wooden bookshelves that held a good number of leather-bound books mixed with law books. The room smelled of old furnace and cigar smoke. The justice of the peace seemed anxious to get this ritual over, so he could move on to his plans for the evening. He didn't look down at a Bible, but, rather, he looked at a paper script that didn't take him more than three minutes to read. He ended with the usual "By the authority vested in me by the laws of the state of Missouri, I now pronounce you husband and wife." After a quick hug and goodbye to our siblings, we climbed into my prepacked silver Plymouth Duster and headed to Detroit, Michigan. It was Friday night, and by Sunday, we would be moving in with Tony's friend and his family until we saved enough money for an apartment.

♦ ♦ ♦

Monday morning, Tony climbed into his friend's truck, and the tires crunched the hardened snow as they backed down the driveway and headed to their jobs at General Motors.

After I brushed my teeth, I strolled back into the room that Tony and I shared and pulled my makeup bag out of my purse. After I coated my face with foundation and pressed powder, I drew a line across my eyelids with liquid eyeliner and rubbed glossy, light pink lipstick across my lips. Then, I grabbed my roller box and unwound my hair from large rollers. After a bit of backcombing, I used the end of the rat-tail comb to lift and fluff. Then, I slipped into a loose-fitting maternity blouse and denim maternity jeans and moseyed out into the living room.

The couple had young kids who were outgoing enough to voice their opinions as to what they wanted to watch on TV but respectful enough to settle into a show without complaint. When the wife saw me, she beamed and gave me a sincere "Good morning." She turned and continued to pick up toys and clothes. After that, she scurried into the kitchen to pour Cocoa Puffs into bowls and apple juice into small glasses. When I sat at the kitchen table and reached for a cigarette, she immediately searched the back of the lower cabinets for an ashtray. The three-bedroom, one-bath house was homey and noisy.

It was about 10:00 a.m. when we heard truck tires, once again, crunch the hardened snow. I traipsed to the front window, and my mouth fell open. I turned to the wife as she gave me a sort of sad smile and looked away. A minute later, Tony marched through the door and told me to "get my shit." The wife corralled her kids into the bedroom, and the friend stood back.

"You told me you had a job!" I turned to his friend. "And *you* verified to me that he *had* a job!"

The friend jerked his head back and gave me a blank stare.

"Just get packed and let's go," Tony said as he marched toward the bedroom.

My heart pounded, and my hands shook as I thundered, "You know I would never have married you if I had known!"

At this point, the wife tilted her head and narrowed her eyes as her husband asked, "What do you mean you would never *have* married him?"

"I *mean* I would never have married him on Friday if I'd known he didn't have a job here." My lips began to tremble, and my breathing increased.

"You mean you just got married on Friday?" His posture collapsed, and he rubbed his chin. "Just this last Friday?"

My words stumbled over each other as I tried to explain. His jaw clenched, and he turned to Tony. "You said you were married!"

Tony jerked my arm, and I yanked it back and planted myself on the couch folding my arms across my chest.

"I'm not going anywhere," I said. Tony's nostrils flared, and he held up his chin before he bolted toward our bedroom. He hurled the suitcase on the bed and tossed in various clothes and belongings. When he returned to the living room, he set the suitcase by the door and headed in my direction. My face turned ashen and I whispered, "Don't come near me."

Tony pointed his finger in my face. "You're coming and we're leaving." He stomped toward the door, and as he passed his friend, he pointed his finger at him and added, "And *you* mind your own god-damn business."

Tony picked up the suitcase and traipsed out the front door. The storm door slammed, and he continued toward the car. When he opened the car door, he looked back at the front door and didn't see me. At that point, his friend slowly took a step outside and onto the front porch pointing his shotgun at Tony.

"She doesn't have to go if she doesn't want to." I slipped out the front door and stood behind Tony's friend.

Tony froze, looked down the barrel of the shotgun, and then his eyes met mine. After several seconds, he set the suitcase on the curb, climbed into the Plymouth Duster, and turned the key.

# CHAPTER THREE

Tony was not quite twenty years old when he drove back down the icy highways of Michigan. He was born into a family that consisted of several boys and one girl. A few of the boys would gather around their mother's kitchen table early every workday morning to debate, argue, consult, and gossip. The room was filled with emotions of all sorts be it bursts of laughter at some off-colored joke or shouts of joy at yesterday's accomplishments or arguments over whose idea it was. Their thick-waisted, gray-haired mother stood in front of the stove as she watched over sizzling bacon, scrambled eggs, or mixed up some sort of savory concoction. Every day after the boys left to do whatever laborious job they had lined up for that day, she would mop the kitchen floor. I once asked Tony how they all lived in such a small house. "Lots of bunk beds," he said with a playful grin.

I was told that it was Tony's dad who discovered that railroad ties made a perfect enclosure for the well-kept gardens of the wealthy;

as a result, railroad ties were in high demand. The boys just had to find used railroad ties, load them onto a rented flatbed truck, and sell them for three dollars each. This type of innovation and hard work produced boys with creative minds, strong backs, loyalty to each other, and few scruples.

◆ ◆ ◆

At twenty-two, I hadn't thought through the logistics of living with strangers in a strange house in a strange town. Reality hit when I saw the wife's eyes sparkle and her husband's face glow after they used their credit card to buy groceries. As soon as they placed several sacks of groceries on the kitchen table, the kids screamed and jumped up and down as they searched through the bags for treats. *The last thing these people need is another mouth to feed,* I thought.

I answered the phone the next time Tony called, and he drove to Michigan and onto his friend's snow-packed driveway. I stared down at my feet as I lugged the suitcase across the sidewalk and climbed into the Plymouth Duster.

A couple of days later, I sat between Tony and his younger brother, and we all bounced up and down in the rented flatbed truck as we hunted for discarded railroad ties. Used railroad ties were left in heaps beside any one of the railroad tracks that zigzagged through Kansas City. Sometimes, I rubbed my hand over my rounded belly and bit my lip as I stared out the window. I wondered what these two brothers would be doing when I was at home taking care of the baby.

◆ ◆ ◆

A few weeks later, Tony pulled into a parking space of a new apartment complex. The mass of brand-new apartments had large, brown-shingled roofs that dipped down over the front of white apartments. In the center of each white apartment unit was a red entry door that was surrounded by brick. My eyes narrowed and my brow wrinkled as he pulled keys out of his pocket and jingled them in front of my eyes. Tony seemed unable to control the smile that spread across his face. My chest tightened, and my face grimaced. I got out of the car and followed him.

"How in the hell are we going to pay for this?" He didn't respond but continued to traipse ahead of me.

We entered the red outer door, and Tony immediately unlocked the first apartment door on the left. The smells of new wood, new shag carpeting, and fresh paint permeated throughout the kitchen, living room, hallway, and two bedrooms.

"Why would you rent something like this without even telling me?" I asked. He just stepped into the kitchen to peer inside new cabinets, a new refrigerator, and a new oven that was underneath the shiny stove top with circular electric burners.

"Don't worry about it." He shrugged his shoulders and headed back to the two bedrooms and two bathrooms.

"Don't worry about it? Why *wouldn't* I worry about paying for a brand-new apartment with a new baby coming and hospital bills?" I followed him through the apartment. He was still grinning when I heard him murmur something about wanting his brothers to see this. I stopped talking, and my mouth snapped shut.

Looking back, I can understand why a new apartment was important to him. He was raised in a small house with a boatload of siblings. On the other hand, I was raised in a brand-new house with three bathrooms and four bedrooms. I knew that lots of money didn't equate to happiness—but he didn't know that. I seemed to always be attracted to boys who lived in two-bedroom, one-bathroom homes because they always seemed to contain families who talked and laughed. When I would drive by enormous houses, I wondered at the debt and the misery trapped inside.

♦ ♦ ♦

The delivery room reeked of Betadine and strong disinfectants that were used to scrub every inch of hospital floors. Masked doctors and attendants with white netting on their heads were in and out as I was sprawled out on a narrow bed with my legs propped up. No one had told me about the pain or anything else having to do with actual childbirth. So, during bouts of torture, I let out gut-wrenching screams and cussed at everyone around me. One blue-robed attendant curled his lip, lowered his eyebrows, and said, "You're right; I'm a man, and I've never been through this." Finally, Jenny cried and it was over.

♦ ♦ ♦

After they wheeled me into my assigned room, I put on my pink, silky nightgown and laid the matching robe across the end of the bed.

After I settled into the bed, they placed Jenny in my arms. She felt weighty even though she only weighed six pounds and twelve ounces.

There were two beds in our room with a small table between us that held a pitcher of water, a couple of glasses, and an ashtray. Hospitals in those days had strict rules about mothers not smoking when the baby was in the room. I took the four-ounce bottle of Similac from the nurse, wedged it into Jenny's mouth, and waited—and waited. I began to swirl the nipple around her lips and rubbed my fingers under her chin. That worked a little, but after thirty minutes, there were still three ounces left in the bottle. Not long after that, the white-capped nurse dressed in a white starched knee-length uniform bounced into the room, grabbed the clipboard that hung on the end of my bed, examined the contents of the bottle, and wrote down the amount. At another time, I noticed that someone had written "failure to thrive" on her chart.

Because Jenny was such a slow eater, we didn't leave the hospital for six days rather than the usual four days. A nurse wheeled me to the front door of KU Medical Center, and Tony opened the door of the Plymouth Duster for me. I clambered into the front passenger seat with Jenny on my lap, and we headed to the apartment that we couldn't afford. We pulled into the parking lot, and Tony had a bounce in his step as he unloaded all the baby items while I put bottles of hospital formula in the refrigerator and sheets and blankets in the bassinet that I'd set beside the double bed.

As I was putting away this and that, Tony mentioned something about meeting his brother for work. "What time do you think you'll be back?"

He shrugged his shoulders as he grabbed the car keys off the kitchen counter. "Don't really know." With a wink and a smile, he strutted out the front door.

# CHAPTER FOUR

Three years earlier, my parents moved to Virginia because my dad had taken a promotion in Washington, D.C. Looking back, I understand my mom better. All through my teenage years, I screamed at her, rolled my eyes, and breathed deeply before I swung around and stomped out of the room. My resentment toward my mom began when I was thirteen and my sister, Vicki, was fifteen. One evening, we stood in the pink-tiled bathroom that smelled of new construction mixed with hairspray and face powder. We communicated back and forth through our reflections in the large bathroom mirror. She stood with her shoulders back, chest out, and chin high as she dabbed makeup on her face and fussed with her short, dark hair.

"Mom is so nice tonight," I said. "She loved brushing my hair and talking to me."

Vicki didn't take her eyes off her own reflection as she applied mascara. "The only time she loves *anyone* is when she's drunk."

With wide eyes, I took a step back, and my body froze. Vicki glanced at my reaction, turned back, and continued to fix herself as if nothing had happened. I knew that on many evenings Mom acted funny, but I loved those times because it was during *those* times that she would talk to me and listen to me when I talked to her. I decided to pay attention to see if what Vicki had said was true.

✦ ✦ ✦

At about 5:00 one evening, I wandered into the kitchen and pulled silverware out of the drawer. Barbeque round steak sizzled in the oven, and baked potatoes wrapped in aluminum foil sat beside them. Mom trotted into the kitchen, glanced through the glass on the oven door, and tied an apron around her tiny waist. She mixed two kinds of liquor and poured it into a long-stemmed glass. With a fork, she dug an olive out of a jar and plopped it into the glass. She set the martini on the kitchen counter, pulled a saucepan out of a lower kitchen cabinet, filled it half full with cold water, set it on the stove, and turned the knob. Mom's makeup was flawless, and her dark hair was styled in a picture-perfect French roll. She grabbed a bag of frozen peas from the freezer and spotted me watching her as I stood by the table with silverware in my hand.

"Jackie, after you set the table, you need to get out of the kitchen while I finish dinner."

I shrugged, folded a napkin, placed the fork on top of it on the left side of the plate, and set the knife and spoon on the right side of the plate. I did this five times and left.

Two hours later, Vicki and I finished the dishes, and I strolled through the family room toward my bedroom. Mom's hair stuck out every which way, and she acted funny as she got up and changed the channel on the TV. When she saw me, Mom smiled and patted the seat next to her. I jerked back and my eyebrows drew together.

"Come sit by me," she said. When I shook my head no, she flinched and the color drained from her face. I just swung my head around, stomped back to my room, and pulled my diary off the top shelf of my closet. I wrote things like "I hate her" and "She's nothing but a drunk" and "Mom was drunk again tonight." A couple of months later, I couldn't find my diary. I climbed on my desk chair and felt all around the upper shelf of my closet, but my diary wasn't there. I took everything off the shelf and rummaged through all my drawers, but I couldn't find my diary anywhere.

Years later, my sister told me that Mom took an overdose of pills when she read my words. But then she threw them back up.

+ + +

A month after I'd brought Jenny home, Tony pounded on the front door. I glanced at the clock—it was midnight. I leaned back on one of the three navy-flowered cushions that lined the back of the navy-blue sofa. I took a drag off my cigarette and crushed it into the mustard-colored ceramic ashtray that overflowed with cigarette butts. More pounding. I trudged toward the door, and with Jenny cradled in my left arm, I turned the doorknob to the right. Before I could open it all the way, Tony fell through the door and onto the floor. His eyes were half closed, and white spittle flowed out of his mouth onto the tiled entryway. The smell of Jim Beam saturated his skin and clothes. Still holding Jenny, I turned and strolled back across the avocado-shag carpet and turned off the static that had begun to emit from the TV. I planted myself back on the sofa and lifted the four-ounce bottle of formula off the end table that held the ceramic ashtray and tall, white-shaded living room lamp. I pressed the nipple between her lips and resumed coaxing her to eat.

I noticed that Tony started to shift to his side and began working his way up the wall to a standing position. I looked down at Jenny and then back up at Tony.

"Where have you been?" No answer. I shook my head and looked back at Jenny. Tony took one step at a time as he tottered through the kitchen and into the dining area. He leaned against the dining room wall and stared at me. I finally lifted my head and glared back. Then, I noticed something on his neck. Keeping my eyes on the spot, I rose from the couch with my left hand wrapped around Jenny and my right hand holding the baby bottle. The nipple was anchored in her mouth. Step by step, I lumbered toward him. I stood silent in front of him with my neck stretched out and my eyes glued to the purplish-red blotch that was pasted to the left side of his neck. I lifted my chin and headed back to my corner of the couch.

"I got it on the dance floor."

"Yeah, right." I looked down at Jenny and shook my head. "You're such an ass."

Tony was somehow able to stumble toward the couch, which made me wonder if all that falling through the door was simply dramatics. He collapsed onto the opposite end of the couch, leaned back on the navy-flowered cushion, and propped his feet up on the wooden coffee table. He tilted his head back and closed his eyes. I continued looking down at Jenny and swirling the nipple around her lips. After a moment, he opened his eyes, sat up, and glowered at me.

"I told you I got it on the dance floor!" He pushed his fingers through his hair and, again, leaned back on the sofa and placed his feet back on the coffee table. Even though my heart was racing, I just stared down at Jenny. For a few moments, the only sound was the air conditioner.

In an instant, I heard the coffee table crash toward the center of the room; and ashtrays, glasses, and other knickknacks hurled into the air before they smashed on the floor and shattered against the wall with a great explosion. I saw Jenny at that moment. With the nipple still in her mouth, she jerked and her face scrunched. Creases appeared between her eyebrows, and her eyes darted in the direction of the blast. Jenny's reaction would be stamped on my brain for the rest of my life. I hurriedly put the bottle on the end table, held her close to my chest, and stood up. At that moment, I realized that it didn't matter if I could live like this. It was not right, and it was unfair to expect my *daughter* to live like this. I turned to Tony. My face burned and my jaw clenched.

"I want you out of here!" I barreled down the hall toward the bedroom. Of course, he wouldn't leave.

## CHAPTER FIVE

When I was about ten and Vicki was about eleven, we would sometimes get up on Sunday mornings and trek two miles to a huge red brick church with four tall white columns lined up in front of white double doors, and all were topped with a pointed white steeple. We found the door for our Sunday School class and entered a room with walls strewed with colorful flowers, crosses, and words like "For God so loved the world." Most of the time, I would look at the other kids and the colorful walls while my sister fixated on the teacher.

Again, about five years later, I stood in Vicki's pink-tiled bathroom and watched her reflection in the bathroom mirror. She leaned her head back with her mouth open as she brushed black mascara through her eyelashes and then she dusted powder on her face. She listened half-heartedly to my babble, and for some reason, we got on the subject of God.

"I used to believe in all that," Vicki said as she picked up her rat-tail comb and used the stem to lift and style the top of her hair. "But I outgrew it."

I flinched and my eyes widened. "You don't believe in God anymore?"

"I used to, but I'm too old for all that now." She stood up straight scanning her reflection in the mirror and then strutted out of the bathroom. I stood completely still and watched her leave. *How can you outgrow God?*

◆ ◆ ◆

After I told Tony to get out, I laid Jenny in her bassinet beside the bed, climbed into our double bed, and stared at the ceiling. My mind raced as I mentally drew up a plan. Tony drove around in my 1971 gray metallic Plymouth Duster as if it were his. It was only a year old, so I could sell it and buy two cheap cars. That way he would have transportation, and I could get a job and a babysitter for Jenny. Eventually, my heart stopped racing, and I closed my eyes and recited the Lord's Prayer.

In less than a month, the Duster was gone, and two used Volkswagen Beetles sat in the parking lot. The red one was in a little better shape, so I made sure Tony had that one, and I drove the yellow one. In no time at all, I was sitting behind a desk at a small mortgage company, collecting payments and filing papers while a thirty-year-old woman took care of Jenny for eight hours a day.

◆ ◆ ◆

When my sister, Vicki, went to the University of Missouri, she rented a room in a sizable old house owned by Mrs. Lindsey. The extra income of $50 a month for each of her three extra bedrooms made a tidy sum for a sixty-year-old widow. My sister was married now, but after another spat with Tony, I called her asking about renting a room from Mrs. Lindsey. Vicki called, and with a bit of persuading, she was able to get Jenny and me into one of Mrs. Lindsey's rooms.

After Tony left to hunt for railroad ties, I packed up and drove to the rented room at Mrs. Lindsey's. I hung up clothes and filled drawers with cloth diapers, plastic pants, and baby pajamas. I found the Southwestern Bell telephone book, and I thumbed through the Yellow Pages under "Attorneys" to find a lawyer who would meet with me.

The following Monday, I took off work early and drove to the attorney's office. It was a balmy September afternoon when I stepped into the modern office building and rode an elevator filled with soft instrumental music to the second floor. After introducing myself to a blond lady at the front desk, I pulled up a chair across from a fortysomething-year-old man who sat behind a wooden desk with a small shaded lamp on one side and a black rotary phone on the other. An ashtray full of cigarette butts sat close to his right hand, and in the middle were papers scattered here and there with a pen laying across them. He sat back comfortably in his chair with his fingers laced together behind his head.

"Just calmly explain that you don't want to argue, but you want a peaceful separation." He uncrossed his fingers and leaned forward as he gave me a knowing grin and a satisfying smile.

"He won't let me do that." I bit my lip and twisted my hair. "He has a bad temper, and he won't listen to me."

He breathed deeply and gave me a dismissive nod as he leaned over his desk and crushed out his cigarette. "He won't be combative if you're not. You just have to let him know you don't want to fight. You want an amicable separation—just for a while."

I grew unusually quiet and stared at the papers on his desk. *Maybe he was right.* I shook his hand, strode out of the office, and drove to the babysitter's white house with green shutters.

◆ ◆ ◆

When my babysitter answered the door, her body stiffened, and she gave me a puzzled stare.

"Your husband picked up Jenny a couple of hours ago."

I froze and my face turned white. "What did he say?"

She suddenly became jumpy and began waving her hands around as she spoke. "I had no idea it would be a problem. He just said he was her father, and he needed to take her home. I didn't think it was a problem."

"Well, it *is* a problem," I murmured. I turned and sprinted toward the car.

◆ ◆ ◆

I knew where Tony would be. I pulled my yellow Volkswagen into the single-car driveway of his mother's house. I turned the key to the off position, and within a minute, Tony jetted through the screen door and dashed toward the car and around to the driver's side. As I rolled down the window, my heart pounded, and my voice shook.

"I just want us to talk—peaceably," I said to his flushed face and clenched jaw. As soon as the window was down far enough, his arm bolted through it and across my chest to wrap his fingers around the car keys. After a quick jiggle, the keys were in his hand and then in his pocket as he headed back into the house. My whole body went limp. I took a deep breath and propped my elbow up on the window sill. My forehead dropped into my left hand, and my fingers blanketed my eyes.

# CHAPTER SIX

I spent most of my high school years trapped in my room. There was no such thing as after-school tutoring to help students who floundered. So every semester, my mom saw the inevitable *D* on my report card, and I was grounded off the phone during the week from 4:00 on. I had to sit at the pink table that my dad had built for me one Christmas and stare at textbooks until I pulled the covers up to my chin that night. On weekends, I was free unless I left clothes on the floor or rolled my eyes and said something like, "That's stupid" or "It's not fair!" Then, on Friday and Saturday nights, I would turn the knob on the pink radio that sat next to my bed, lie down on top of the bedspread, and stare at the ceiling as I listened to The Mamas & the Papas or The Monkees on WHB in Kansas City.

A few months after my eighteenth birthday, I paid an employment agency a month's salary to get a job at an insurance company that paid $250 a month. I was a basket girl. The BMA tower was nineteen floors high and surrounded by walls of enormous glass windows that reached the ceiling. My job was to pick up gold interdepartmental envelopes and other various types of mail from a dumb waiter located in a small room. Then, I matched the name on the envelope to the name on the labeled folder that hung in my little grocery store-type wheeled cart. Every hour, I wheeled around the fifteenth floor, put mail in inboxes, and picked up mail from outboxes. As I dropped off mail for a pudgy, older man in a corner office, I chatted with his young, brown-haired, blue-eyed secretary.

"I'm looking for a roommate," she said.

My eyes widened. I nodded along as she explained her situation. She lived in a room with a private bath on the top floor of an old three-story house, and she needed to split the rent.

I leaned forward. "Really?" Then, I pressed my lips together. "But I don't have a car."

"No problem. I just catch a ride with a gal on the tenth floor."

The corners of my mouth turned up, and my heart felt light. I turned my grocery-mail cart around and continued back down the aisle.

♦ ♦ ♦

Within a few days, I came to blows with my mom. We were standing face to face in front of the fireplace in the family room. Her breath smelled of alcohol, and her hair stuck out everywhere. With a red face and flared nostrils, she told me I couldn't use the phone. I threw my head around flipping my long hair in her face. Before I knew it, her long, red, manicured fingernails wrapped around the hair on the back of my head.

I shrieked and threw my hands behind my head to unlock her grip. I broke loose and scrambled to get to the mustard-yellow wall phone that hung in the hallway. Mom turned in the opposite direction and dashed to the master bedroom to the white rotary phone on her dresser. She knew if she took the receiver off *that* phone, I couldn't call out. I picked up the yellow wall phone receiver and could not get a dial tone.

I sped through the entryway and out the front door into the cool November night. Within seconds, I banged on my neighbor's door. Unlike the house I just left, my neighbor's house was quiet and peaceful. There were no ashtrays in the house, so the air was filled with a fresh, clean fragrance. A pastel-pink floral sofa was centered in the room, and a cream-colored Queen Anne chair sat in the corner. Lamps with white, bell-shaped shades gave a soft glow to the perfectly arranged living room. Our neighbor jerked her head back when she saw my face. When I regained my composure, I asked to use the phone.

I dialed my boyfriend to ask if he could come get me and my girlfriend to see if I could stay with her that night. I put the receiver back on the wall phone in the kitchen and stepped into my neighbor's living room. With a strained voice, I asked her if I could wait there for a while. She nodded her head, gave me a soft smile, and strolled to the back of the house.

◆ ◆ ◆

When my boyfriend arrived, we strolled back to my house. I opened the front door, and we stepped into the entryway. I turned to my boyfriend. "Wait here."

Immediately, my dad bellowed. "Get in here!" He emerged from the family room with a scowl on his face.

"I'm leaving," I said. I headed down the hall, and my dad sprang into action and set off after me.

My boyfriend took a couple of steps forward. "Mr. Clark, how do you expect her to live in a house like this?"

Dad turned with blazing eyes and an outstretched finger. "From this point forward, you are no longer welcome in this house."

"Wait in the car!" I said as I continued toward my bedroom.

My dad traipsed into my room. "Just come sit down for a minute, and let's talk about this." He patted the bed. My face burned as tears of anger cascaded down my cheeks, and my body shook uncontrollably. He tried to put his arm around me, but I just kept scooting down the bed trying to get away from him.

"Jackie, just leave for tonight and come back tomorrow." I nodded my head and finished gathering my stuff.

The next day, I went home and packed the rest of my things while my mom and dad stayed in the kitchen. Afterward, I went into the kitchen. My parents were unusually quiet. Mom stood at the kitchen counter concentrating on whatever she was doing, and Dad slouched back on a kitchen chair with his right foot resting on his left knee. His arm stretched across the table with a cigarette in his hand. I stood there for a few moments, but nothing was said except unimportant small talk. With nothing left to say, I turned around, went through the family room, down the front entryway, and out the front door.

◆ ◆ ◆

I continued to sit in my yellow Volkswagen on Tony's mom's driveway. After several moments, I let out a long, low sigh and mustered the energy to get out of the car and amble toward the back screen door to get Jenny and face Tony.

He sat on the couch, and his gaunt face stared down at his hands. I reached for Jenny, held her close to my chest, and sat down. He didn't want a divorce, and I didn't want to keep fighting. I couldn't live with the constant worry about what he was doing with his brothers, and he couldn't do his job without them.

I thought about the fact that Tony's brothers were here, but *my* dad's family lived in Wichita. *If we move to Wichita, I'll have aunts and uncles to call if I need them,* I thought.

My face started to light up. "You could get a job in Wichita, and we could move *there*."

Tony studied my face and gently bit his lip.

I continued, "Wichita is only a three-hour drive from here, so you'd still be pretty close to your family."

After a couple of minutes, Tony swallowed hard and gave me a half-smile. "Let's do it."

# CHAPTER SEVEN

By the first part of October, both the red and yellow Volkswagens were in Wichita and parked in front of a two-bedroom blond-brick duplex. Tony held one end of the navy-blue sofa, and I held the other as we trudged up the long sidewalk under a cloudy sky. After we lugged in the matching navy chair, the two-chair dinette table, a dresser, and the end tables, we set the mattress on top of the frame for the double bed. Tony put screws in the white crib while I dug through boxes, sorted through clothes, towels, and dishes, and found a home for each item.

We weren't there a whole week when Tony started in about moving back to Kansas City. I poured formula into a glass bottle, set it in a pan of water, and turned the knob on the stove. After testing the temperature of the formula by shaking a few drops on my wrist, I sat on one of the two chairs at the dinette table, lit a cigarette, and laid Jenny across my lap. When I put the nipple in her mouth, she sucked without prompting—finally. Tony stomped back and forth across the living room.

"I can make a lot more money with railroad ties than working at any stupid job around here." I shifted in my chair and glanced toward him.

"Then leave." I reached for my cigarette, took a drag, and murmured, "You're such a jerk."

I turned back and focused on Jenny.

His voice became steady and low-pitched. "If I go, you're going with me."

I looked up from Jenny and glared at him with my jaw set. "No—I won't."

His eyes locked with mine for a couple of moments. Then he grabbed his keys off the coffee table and sneered as he shook his head. He slammed the front door behind him, and a moment later, I heard the engine of his red Volkswagen rev up and then fade away as he set out toward the Kansas Turnpike.

I sat for a few minutes before I noticed the back door. I set the bottle on the table and smashed out my cigarette in the ashtray before getting up and situating Jenny over my shoulder. I rubbed her back as I took a couple of steps to the backdoor and opened it. Sunshine and a fragrant breeze flowed through the back screen door. I could feel my lips break into a smile and my eyes light up as I settled back into the chair and placed the nipple back into Jenny's mouth. For the next hour, I gazed through that screen door and enjoyed the fading grass, the rustling leaves—and freedom.

◆ ◆ ◆

After Tony left, I paid a visit to my Aunt Lee that same afternoon. Aunt Lee was five years younger than my dad, and she was the youngest child among four children. She had short brown hair, a thin frame, and a quick wit. All my dad's siblings strove for success, and they laughed a lot along the way.

When Aunt Lee opened the door, her eyes went past me and straight to Jenny. After an "Oh my goodness!" she reached out to hold her and gushed phrases like "She's such a pretty baby!" and "How old is she now?" Her excitement made my nervous heart slow down and my shoulders relax.

Aunt Lee's ten-year-old, white, split-level house held memories of Vicki and me sharing secrets and giggles in the back bedroom with our two cousins. Her two daughters were close to our age, but now they were both grown and gone, and her teenage son was tucked away in his bedroom upstairs.

Aunt Lee laid Jenny in my arms, reached for a Coke from the refrigerator, and handed it to me. She led me into the adjacent living room that smelled of smoke and freshly vacuumed carpet. She waved her hand toward the brown and gold, flowered sofa as a gesture for me to sit. I set the Coke on the end table and spread out a pink blanket on the sofa for Jenny to lie on. Aunt Lee settled into a nearby velvet gold chair and reached for a cigarette and matchbook from a small end table nearby. After she tore off a match and gave it a quick swipe over the striking surface, she lit her cigarette and mine, shook her hand to put out the fire, and tossed the used match into the ashtray. She lifted her head, blew smoke into the air, and turned to me with the corners of her mouth turned up. "Well, what's going on, girl?"

I jabbered on and on for almost an hour before I told her that Tony had gone back to Kansas City that morning, and I was scared he would come back. I wiped my clammy hands on my jeans. "He has a key to my apartment." Aunt Lee figured out that I needed money and some sort of protection.

"How much do you think you'll need?" she said as she smashed out her cigarette in the ashtray beside her chair.

"Since I already have a car and an apartment, I just need money until I get a job." I bit my lips. "I will pay you back, I promise."

Aunt Lee nodded. When she was young, she was left with two daughters and had to get help from my grandmother. She strolled to the entryway toward her purse and pulled out her checkbook. "Do you have a number in mind?" Aunt Lee squeezed my shoulder on her way back to her chair.

I avoided eye contact and shifted in my seat. "Since the rent's paid for this month, maybe a hundred dollars for gas and food."

She scribbled numbers on a check, ripped it out, and handed it to me.

"I really, really appreciate this," I said as I reached for my purse. I stuck the check lengthwise inside the dollar pocket of my billfold and put it back inside my purse. She knew all about my relationship with my mom, and she knew her brother, my dad, could not be counted on to come through in a situation like this.

◆ ◆ ◆

A short time later, Uncle Bill came home, gave Aunt Lee a quick peck, and acknowledged Jenny. We got through the congenial small talk, and he pulled up another chair. Aunt Lee explained my fears, and he listened with a serious demeanor and thoughtful expression. I knew he was mentally creating a solution to the problem of keeping Tony out of my apartment.

The next day, he brought his tool kit, a metal bar, and two brackets to my apartment. It didn't take him long to hammer in one metal bracket on one side of the door frame and the other metal bracket on the other side. He then told me that every time I came home, I needed to close the door and just slide the metal bar down and onto the top of the brackets.

"There is no way he's going to get through that door," he said with a wink and a grin.

Unfortunately, Uncle Bill didn't take into consideration that it would only work when I was *inside* the apartment.

# CHAPTER EIGHT

When I used to wheel my grocery-mail cart around the fifteenth floor of the BMA tower, I would pass by ladies whose desks were lined up beside a long gray partition. Those ladies wore earphones, and their fingers clicked away on electric typewriters. Fluorescent bulbs lit the entire floor, and the smell of cigarette smoke routinely mingled with Charlie perfume from the ladies who worked near the corner offices or at desks topped with calculators. Some of those ladies would stride by with their chins held high while others wore red lipstick and long earrings and would laugh and tease the men dressed in suits and ties who sat at the desks behind the partition.

The ladies alongside the gray partition were called stenographers, and they would stop periodically to rewind the tape in the cassette recorder that sat on their desk to make sure they heard correctly. The underwriters, who worked behind the partition, were the ones who made the recordings.

FOR THE LOVE OF GOD

I wanted to be a stenographer, but I had to pass a typing test that required typing forty words a minute with no more than five errors. Accuracy was important because it took so much time to correct a mistake. If a stenographer typed a *d* instead of an *e*, she would have to stop, pick up a small strip of white correction tape, place it between the black ribbon and the letterhead paper, and retype the *d* to cover it up with white. Then, she would reach for a pencil eraser, lift up the bar on the typewriter, and reach behind the letterhead to erase the *d* from each of the carbon copies. Now she was ready to make the correction. She would pull the bar back down over the letterhead paper, line up the empty space, and hit the *e* key several times.

There was a typewriter on an empty desk that sat alongside the partition, and between mail runs, I would sit and practice. Several times I rode the elevator down to the Personnel Department, took the typing test, and stepped out with a typing test full of circled errors. I made myself lift my sagging head and return to my seat in front of the typewriter.

Mr. Martin was probably about fifty or sixty years old, balding, and on the heavy side. He was the head of the whole department, and his office was in the corner. If he walked by me while I was practicing and I happened to look up, he would smile down at me. One day he stopped.

"You should try to be accurate and not worry about typing fast. I would suggest you slow way down and focus on accuracy. Your speed will come naturally with practice, so don't worry about that." He grinned, patted my shoulder, and headed back to his office.

I watched his back as he strolled toward his office, and I turned back to my typewriter. I began to type at a rate of one click per second. When people strutted by me, I could feel my face burn, but I kept at this measured pace. The next time I took a typing test, I passed. Before long, I wore earphones and sat at my own desk topped with a typewriter and cassette player.

◆ ◆ ◆

A couple of days after Uncle Bill installed the brackets and bars, I sat down at the kitchen table and figured out my money. I had made about $440.00 a month when I left BMA, but no new job would pay that kind of money. After I listed all my expenses and possible future expenses, I figured that I could make it, barely, on $320.00 a month.

I laid the newspaper want ads on the kitchen table and circled office jobs that required typing and filing. After calling and getting addresses, I loaded Jenny into the yellow Volkswagen and drove to the first possibility.

At the first circled location, I entered through a glass door in a strip mall and asked the receptionist about the office job in the newspaper. The blond-haired, thirtysomething-year-old lady raised her eyebrows when she spotted Jenny and paused. She looked back at me and asked if I could type. When I said yes, she handed me an application attached to a brown clipboard. I glanced around and found an empty place beside a brown metal folding chair, so I set the carrier down and laid Jenny in it. I filled in the blanks on the application form that asked about my age, weight, marital status, previous employment, and hobbies. After I handed it to the receptionist, I picked up Jenny and the carrier and followed her into a small room with a chair facing a typewriter and a sheet of paper beside it titled "Typing Test 5 Minutes." After I settled in front of the typewriter, the blond-haired lady hit the timer and strode back to her desk. After she graded my test and wrote the results on my application, she handed it back to me and tossed my application on a stack of others. I opened the door of my yellow Volkswagen, placed Jenny and her yellow carrier in the passenger's seat, and picked up the typing test. I saw three circled errors and the words *60 WPM* written on the top of the page. My face glowed as I wiggled into the driver's seat, leaned toward the steering wheel, and turned the key.

◆ ◆ ◆

At about 5:00 or 6:00 p.m., I pulled in front of the blond duplex and stepped out of the car into fall-like weather and an overcast sky. I strolled around to the passenger side, reached in to lift Jenny out of her carrier, and grabbed her diaper bag off the floor. My hands were loaded, so I struggled to match the key to the keyhole. Finally, I gave the key a twist and stepped through the door of my apartment. I knew what the rustling sound was that came from the back bedroom. Blood drained from my face and I froze.

"It's all right," Tony said, "it's just me." I flinched and stepped back as my eyes widened. *Did he really think those words would provide some sort of comfort?*

"Why are you here?" I laid Jenny down on the couch and began unpinning her diaper.

"I wanna talk," he said.

"There's nothing to talk about." I covered her diaper with plastic pants and took the wet diaper to the hamper in her room. Tony watched Jenny as I headed to the kitchen, placed a pan of water on the stove, and turned on the heat.

Through the next hour or two, neither of us yelled or got mad. He wanted me to go back to Kansas City, and I said no. He didn't say much as he sat on the couch, and I fed Jenny. After about forty-five minutes, I held her to my chest and rubbed her back before laying her on the couch beside Tony while I went to the kitchen to clean up. Finally, he reached for her coat and started to put her arm through the arm of her coat.

"What are you doing?" I darted out of the kitchen and extended my hand and arm between him and Jenny. He just elbowed me out of the way and finished getting her coat on. He stood, grabbed the pink blanket that was lying beside her, and held her close as he headed toward the door. I followed him toward the door with a stunned look on my face.

"Where are you going?" I quickly glanced at the door and then back at Tony with his arms anchored around Jenny.

"I'll be back," he said. "I'm just going to buy her some toys." It was dark outside when he opened the door, and cold air rushed into the apartment. I watched Tony walk with wide steps toward his red Volkswagen.

After I closed the door, I felt my whole body draw in as I sat down on the navy couch and wrapped my arms around myself.

✦ ✦ ✦

It was about an hour later when I tapped on Aunt Lee's door. She immediately called the police, and within minutes, a policeman was sitting on a chair with an end table and lamp beside him. Aunt Lee sat on the brown and gold floral sofa, and she leaned toward him with her elbows on her knees and her hands folded under her chin. Her eyes fixated on him, and her ears attended to his every word. I was off to the side sitting on the edge of a corner chair with my hands on my knees and a burning cigarette on a table close by. As the policeman and Aunt Lee conversed, my head turned back and forth between them.

"Can't you arrest him for kidnapping?" Aunt Lee said.

"He's the *father*," the policeman reiterated. He shifted in his seat under Aunt Lee's glare and relentless questioning.

"What the hell! She's the mother, and she's been taking care of the baby the entire time!" Aunt Lee stood up, threw her hands up in the air, and her face reddened. "Are you telling me you're not going to do *anything*?"

My hands felt clammy and my voice shook when I interjected, "You can call someone and stop him right now. He's on the Kansas Turnpike headed toward Kansas City."

The policeman jerked and blinked. "It doesn't matter," he said as he bit his lips. "Unless you have legal child custody, there's nothing I can do."

"I can't believe the law would allow a father to just come in and take a child away from her mother, and she can't do a damn thing about it," said Aunt Lee. She shook her head harder and lit another cigarette. "Jenny is just a baby, and mothers *always* get custody of a baby."

Finally, the policeman just shrugged his shoulders, apologized, and left.

◆ ◆ ◆

After I crawled into bed that night, I said the Lord's Prayer and lay awake. The next day, I went to five different places and filled out five different applications for the receptionists to throw on top of a pile of other filled-out applications. I dialed Tony's mom's house, but no one answered.

That evening, I took the phone book out of the kitchen drawer and found the names of a couple of lawyers from the Yellow Pages and wrote down their names and phone numbers. The wall phone rang, and I picked up the receiver on the first ring. It wasn't Tony—it was Aunt Lee. Her voice was shrill and shaky, and her words didn't make sense. Every once in a while, I caught the words *Tony* and *please* and *custody*. Finally, she made herself say a coherent sentence.

"You have to leave Jenny alone." Her words were stated one word at a time as a simple matter of fact. I pulled out a chair from under the dinette table and sat down.

"I don't understand what you're saying."

"Tony called me, and he called your Uncle Gilbert." She was breathing so hard, I thought she must be hyperventilating. "He told both of us that if you tried to get Jenny, he would harm our children."

"What do you mean he would harm your children?" I didn't fear Tony, but I did fear Aunt Lee. She was petrified and unreasonable.

"He said he would kill them," she said. Aunt Lee pleaded with me to "please leave Jenny alone" and "please don't try to get custody of her."

"Aunt Lee, Tony's not a killer. That's just the way they talk," I said. "One time, his dad told me he was going to put concrete boots on me and throw me into the Missouri River. It doesn't mean anything. He's just mad."

That world was foreign to Aunt Lee, and she didn't hear anything through her panic and shock. "Please, please, please just leave him alone and leave Jenny there," she said.

There was no changing her mind. I felt dizzy, and I struggled to breathe. I muttered something about leaving it alone for now and hung up. With my hand still on the receiver, I spotted the paper with the names and numbers of the two lawyers. After a moment's hesitation, I folded the paper and shoved it to the back of the counter.

# CHAPTER NINE

My dad was seven years old when his forty-two-year-old father died. His dad (my grandfather) had been in a hurry to get back to his sewing machine business, so he demanded the dentist remove all his teeth—at once—in his backyard, no less. The next morning, he swallowed arsenic and died. His death left my grandmother (Daisy) with five children to raise during the Great Depression: two girls and three boys.

Most of the siblings were convinced that their father had committed suicide because that's what they had been told. Uncle Gilbert was fourteen years old at the time, and he never offered his opinion. However, the oldest girl, Eva Mae, was thirteen at the time, and she stood firm in her belief that her father would never do that.

Eva Mae was also confrontational about her beliefs in God. She was the only one of the five children to pursue some sort of religion. She badgered her brothers and younger sister (Aunt Lee) about their need to believe in God and Jesus, and she was surprised when they all turned on her. Eventually, Eva Mae and her husband gathered their belongings, loaded up their two daughters, and moved to Long Beach. Eventually, she became the director of Child Evangelism in Orange County.

✦ ✦ ✦

After the phone conversation with Aunt Lee, I felt as if I had fallen into a black pit. For the next couple of weeks, I stumbled through the doors of several small offices in a daze and requested an application. I was in some sort of fog and in a world that I wasn't a part of. I couldn't hear people, and I couldn't see what was in front of me. Several times during an interview, I asked, "I'm sorry; what did you say?" I knew something was wrong, so I tried to solve the problem. I would stop at a stop sign and think, *Look at the sign. See, it's red and white. Focus on what you see around you.* At a stop light, I thought, *See the red light, now watch for it to turn green.* During an interview, I made myself think *Watch the person moving his lips and listen. Keep focused on his words right now.*

After almost two weeks of filling out applications and no job, I pulled up to a temporary agency, filled out the usual forms, and took a typing test. Within a few days, I wandered into an impressive car dealership with a glassed showroom that held a shiny new Pontiac Le Mans, a Mercedes Benz, and a two-door Honda Civic. A giddy, long-haired girl greeted me with a smile and pointed me in the right direction. After I sat down in front of a typewriter, my brown-haired,

red-lipped trainee pointed to sales contracts and title applications that needed to be typed, and she pulled out file drawers as she explained the system. After about thirty minutes, she hurried out, and I rolled the first sales contract into the typewriter, lowered the bar, and began to type. The job paid the minimum wage of $1.60 an hour, which would have amounted to not quite $280.00 a month. That made it $40.00 short of my needed $320.00—but it was something.

♦ ♦ ♦

Aunt Lee sat on the edge of my floral navy-blue couch with a checkbook on her knees and a pen in her hand. It was toward the end of the month, and my rent was due.

"Even though I have that temporary job, I still fill out applications," I said as I fidgeted with the top button of my blouse. "I'm thinking that I should apply at one of the aircraft companies."

The phone rang, and I walked back into the bedroom, sat on the edge of the double bed, and picked up the green receiver. It was Eva Mae, Aunt Lee's religious sister, calling from California. Eva Mae's usual smile in her voice and her quick laugh were gone, and she just asked questions. How was I? Uncle Gilbert had called her, and she was concerned. She let me know that God would take care of me and that she would pray for me. I knew Eva Mae kept track of the time because every minute on the phone cost her money, and I also knew that Aunt Lee was fidgeting in the next room. I thanked Eva Mae for the call and appreciated her prayers. I put the receiver down and headed back to the living room.

"Who was that?" Aunt Lee said. When I told her it was Eva Mae, she gave a heavy sigh and sneered. "What did she say?"

"She just said she was sorry I was having a hard time, and she would pray for me."

Aunt Lee grimaced and her eyes narrowed. "I'll tell you what. Why don't you tell her that next time, *she* can write the checks, and *I'll* pray!"

She stared at me and waited for me to agree with her. I liked Eva Mae, and I didn't want to get in the middle of this sibling rivalry, so I avoided her gaze and fidgeted with my fingernails. Aunt Lee just shook her head, looked back at her checkbook, and finished filling out the check.

❖ ❖ ❖

By the end of the next week, I drove my yellow Volkswagen into the parking lot of the corporate office for Cessna Aircraft Company. The receptionist handed me an application to fill out and told me I had to take a typing test. She glanced over the application, made a note of my typing score, and had me sit back down. Before long, she called my name, and I entered a small office with a pudgy, middle-aged man seated behind a desk with a cigarette hanging out of his mouth. He wore a short-sleeved white shirt that had the top button undone and a disheveled tie he had loosened from around his neck. He leaned over a desk with stacks of papers scattered here and there, and he smashed out his cigarette in an ashtray overflowing with cigarette butts.

"Are you married?" he asked as he leaned back in his chair and skimmed over my application.

"No, I'm getting a divorce," I said. "I have a daughter." *Keep your mind focused. Listen closely*, I thought.

"Do you have any physical disability?"

"No." I shifted in my chair and pulled down my skirt.

"We have an opening in the Quality Assurance Department." He leaned forward on his desk. "Are you interested?"

I was at a loss for words, and I looked at him with wide eyes. "How much money, uh—I mean, how much is the pay?"

"Well, let's see." He picked up his reading glasses and reached across his desk to a particular group of papers. He plucked out one page and held it up to his face. "It looks as if you'll start at $540.00 a month."

# CHAPTER TEN

It had been about five weeks since Tony called Aunt Lee and Uncle Gilbert, so I went into the kitchen and retrieved the piece of paper I had slid to the back of the counter. I dialed the number of the first attorney and made an appointment to see him the next day.

Marlin's office had the smell of furniture polish mixed with English Leather cologne, and his bookshelves contained textbooks and lawbooks. His wooden desk held a brass desk lamp that was centered directly over folders, and an unused glass ashtray had been scooted off to the side. When I first strode into his office, he was leaning back in a leather chair and flipping through papers that were stapled together. When Marlin looked up from his papers, he quickly put the papers on his desk, stood up, and buttoned the bottom of his suit jacket as he stepped out from behind his desk and held out his hand. Marlin was twenty-six years old and had dark hair and blue eyes. He was short, stocky, and confident.

I sat down on the chair in front of his desk and lit a cigarette. He slid the glass ashtray toward me. "What can I do for you?"

He nodded as I rattled on about Tony taking Jenny to Kansas City and how he threatened Aunt Lee and Uncle Gilbert, and I didn't know what I could do.

Through the course of the conversation, I learned he had a couple of kids—but his wife would oversleep and she would not get the kids to school on time and he didn't know how he would be able to stay with her. Marlin would sometimes have to leave work and take care of things at home, but he just couldn't do that being a new lawyer and all. We had talked back and forth for about two hours when I leaned toward the ashtray on his desk and smashed out my fourth cigarette. I stared at him as he sat back in his chair with his fingers pressed together in contemplation.

"We could file for custody." He tilted his head and paused. "If you want to—that is."

"I want Jenny, but Aunt Lee has supported me for almost *six weeks*, and she's petrified." I fidgeted with my hands and bit my lips.

Marlin took a deep breath, sat back in his chair, and laced his fingers behind his head. "You'll just have to decide if you want to be a mother or a niece."

My head jerked. A moment later, I relaxed. "How long does it take to get the legal papers?"

◆ ◆ ◆

I told my sixty-year-old landlady, Mrs. Feather, I had to move.

She swiveled her chair around, pulled out a folder from a metal filing cabinet, and laid it on her desk. There was only a one-bedroom available, and it was in a red brick fourplex. The rent was $99.00 a month.

Although it was cold outside, it was warm inside, and I hummed and grinned as Uncle Bill (Aunt Lee's husband) helped me move my double bed, end table, and Jenny's white crib along the front windowed wall of the lone bedroom. He then set the upright wooden dresser along a side wall. In the living room, the navy-blue, floral sofa and end table fit along the inside wall, and we set the wooden coffee table in front of it. The front door and double windows were on the front wall of the living room, and one of the windows held the window air conditioner. We grunted and groaned as we maneuvered the wooden TV cabinet through the door and lined it up along the wall opposite the sofa. I placed the dinette table with two chairs in the small eating space beside the galley kitchen. After Uncle Bill left, I clanged around and put dishes in kitchen cabinets, hung blue striped towels over towel racks in the bathroom, and laid a new blue and white flowered bathmat in front of the bathtub. There was no shower, but—still—this apartment was perfect.

❖ ❖ ❖

After our meeting, I began to see Marlin outside the office, and two weeks after filing, we drove to Kansas City. He reminded me that the custody papers were only legal in Kansas, and Tony lived in Missouri.

"Let's hope he doesn't notice," Marlin said as he rolled down his window and took the ticket for the Kansas Turnpike.

"We need to get the sheriff to stand at the front door." I blew cigarette smoke out of the corner of my mouth. "Then, you and I will go around and knock on the back door."

Marlin looked over at me with raised eyebrows. "Why in the world would you want a sheriff at the front door?"

"Because Tony will try to run out the front door." After a moment's silence, I glanced at him and saw his flat gaze. "They do things like that." I crumbled up my empty pack of cigarettes, threw it out the window, and rummaged through my purse for a piece of gum.

Marlin watched me with furrowed eyebrows, shook his head, and looked back at the road.

◆ ◆ ◆

Marlin stood behind me with the folded custody papers in his hand, and I knocked on the back screen door. Tony opened the back door, and his blue eyes widened when he saw me. He shoved the door back in my face and rushed back into the house. I pushed through the door before it closed and barged through the small laundry area and into the kitchen as I shouted and cussed and yelled along the way, but Tony had already rushed past the kitchen into the hall.

Marlin and I remained in the kitchen where four of his brothers sat at the kitchen table with white coffee mugs in front of them. The smell of bacon lingered in the air, and the sink was full of dishes with dried egg stuck on plates and empty juice glasses. The initial outburst and chaos dissipated, and Marlin stood with his shoulders back, chest out, and chin high.

"She has legal custody of Jenny, so he'll have to hand her over," Marlin said as he held up the documents.

Tony appeared with Jenny in his arms, and I reached out to her, but he elbowed me out of the way.

"Tony, don't give her anything," his older brother said. "Call a lawyer." He stood up, stepped around the table, and pulled a phone book out of a drawer. After a brief conversation with a Missouri lawyer, they told us to leave.

◆ ◆ ◆

When we were back in Marlin's car, he saw black mascara running down my face and assured me this was not over. He turned the keys and looked over his shoulder with his right arm stretched across the back of my seat as he backed out of the driveway and headed downtown toward the courthouse. On the way, he talked about filing a petition for a writ of habeas corpus and finding a judge to sign it.

The next morning, the signed writ of habeas corpus lay on the dash of the car, and snow blanketed the ground when we pulled up to Tony's mom's house. Although it was cold, Tony waited at the edge of the sidewalk and wore only a long-sleeved blue shirt. He had one arm wrapped around a bundle of pink and white blankets with Jenny buried inside. The yellow baby carrier and bags of baby clothes, diapers, and various other baby items lay on the ground beside him. With shoulders slumped and dull eyes, he laid Jenny in my arms.

For the love of god

"She has a doctor's appointment later this week. All the information is right here." Tony pointed to an appointment card on top of one of the bundles. I ignored him as Marlin and I gathered her things into the car and sat her in the baby carrier in the backseat.

"Please keep the doctor's appointment." His hands trembled and his face blanched. Tony didn't look at Marlin and he didn't look at me and he didn't ask for the legal papers. The only thing he cared about was that I kept Jenny's doctor's appointment. Since it seemed so important to him, I said I would, but that was the last time I thought about it. Within minutes we were back on the Kansas Turnpike headed to Wichita. I would soon learn why that appointment was so important.

# CHAPTER ELEVEN

Aunt Lee set me up on a payment plan to pay back the money I owed her. It wasn't the whole amount, but it was enough to satisfy her and relieve my conscience. After two weeks of hounding, Aunt Lee finally talked me into taking Jenny to Dr. Robinson. I didn't see why I needed to take her to the doctor, but to appease Aunt Lee, I made an appointment.

Aunt Lee and I strolled into the pediatric waiting room with walls lined with metal-legged, gray-padded chairs and an overflowing toy box in the corner. It smelled of toddler diapers and vacuumed Berber carpet. Moms sat in chairs with eyes glued to kids clanging multicolored toys, and, periodically, one would tell their two-year-old to "Come sit by me" or "Get away from that." Magazines and ashtrays lay on top of end tables. I gave my name to the brown-haired, middle-aged receptionist who sat behind the check-in counter, and she handed me a clipboard full of forms with a pen stuck under the top of the clipboard. After filling out all the personal information, I pulled out my new insurance card that I had just received from Cessna and wrote all the appropriate numbers in all the appropriate boxes.

Before long, a nurse dressed in a white uniform and white hat directed us to a room with a small examination table and a couple of chairs.

"Dr. Robinson will be with you in a few minutes," she said. "Just take off all Jenny's clothes, except her diaper, and lay her clothes at the end of the table." Her mouth curved up into a smile as she stepped out.

The room felt sterile and clean. Diplomas from the KU School of Medicine lined the white walls, and a small table off to the side held a lamp, Kleenex, and cotton balls. Aunt Lee sat on the chair and chatted with me as I took off Jenny's pink and white snow coat and lacy light blue dress. I folded everything and stacked them just so at the end of the table with her socks and white shoes.

When Dr. Robinson entered the room, he introduced himself and stretched out his hand to me and Aunt Lee. He had dark balding hair, brown eyes, and a serious, yet approachable, demeanor. He knew Aunt Lee, and they conversed about her grandchildren. After the niceties, everyone was quiet as Dr. Robinson held Jenny's head as he sat her up and pressed the stethoscope to her chest and back. He laid her down on her back and took out a small instrument to look in her ears, and then he waved a small flashlight around her eyes. Dr. Robinson continued pressing, turning, looking, and listening while Aunt Lee leaned against the doorway with her arms folded over her chest and her head down and tilted. No one said anything. Eventually, Dr. Robinson stopped and backed away as he put his instruments away and picked up a folder for notes. Aunt Lee's eyebrows drew together, and she broke the silence.

"Dr. Robinson, do you think she's blind?" My mind began to unravel. *Blind? Where did that come from?*

"Yes, I think she's blind, and she'll probably never walk and never talk, and I think you should put her in an institution."

Even though my heart stopped beating and my insides caved in, I made myself stand up, unfold Jenny's dress, and begin to dress her. My head felt heavy, and my mind was buried in a deep fog. In the background, far away, I heard tiny voices conversing, and they wouldn't shut up, and I didn't want to hear them. All I could think was, *I have to get out of here,* and *they're going to make me put her in an institution.* As I struggled to get Jenny's arms through small, lacy armholes, I noticed that drops of water fell, one after another, from my face and onto her blue dress. After an eternity, her coat was zipped, and I was out the door.

♦ ♦ ♦

Not knowing what else to do, I knocked on Uncle Gilbert's door. Uncle Gilbert and Aunt Francie lived in a huge red brick house that was built in the early 1900s. I remember when my sister (Vicki), my cousins, and I would run up the carved wooden staircase from the elegant entryway and then down the narrow back staircase, which was originally the servant's stairway. The sunken living room had a huge black Steinway in the corner, and the cream-colored stucco above the fireplace reached the ceiling and had a *C* for *Clark* chiseled into it. Aunt Francie had majored in home economics in college, so all the furniture, draperies, and knickknacks emitted a sense of sophistication and style. No ashtrays were allowed in the house, so the scent of cleanness and warmth mingled together.

Uncle Gilbert gave me a knowing smile when he opened the door and held it open for me as I carried Jenny and a stuffed diaper bag into the living room. I pulled a blanket out of the diaper bag, spread it out on the living room carpet, and laid Jenny on it. After pinning a clean diaper on her and pulling up her plastic pants, I placed the wet diaper in an empty plastic bread bag and stuffed it back into the diaper bag. After that, I pulled out a bottle of formula and rolled up another cloth diaper to prop it up. I turned Jenny on her side, guided her to the bottle, and she drank quietly and began to close her eyes.

Aunt Francie was in one chair and Uncle Gilbert was in another, and neither of them spoke. I sat back on the sofa and watched Jenny.

"Dr. Robinson said she was blind and would probably never walk or talk, and I needed to put her in an institution," I said. When I looked at them, Aunt Francie was leaning toward me with her elbow on her knee and her hand under her chin. Uncle Gilbert sat back in his chair and gazed at me through wire-rimmed glasses. I wasn't used to people tiptoeing around me, and I didn't understand why they were so quiet and acting like this.

"What do *you* think?" Uncle Gilbert said.

"I don't want to." I sighed, leaned my head back on the back of the sofa, and stared at the ceiling. "I think they said something about how an institution is probably the best place for her." Aunt Francie studied my face.

After a few moments, she sat up in her chair as if she had just remembered something. "It seems as if there is some sort of service for the blind here in Kansas," she said. "They might be able to help you."

I raised my head from the back of the sofa with raised eyebrows. "You mean I could find places to help her?" They glanced at each other and back to me.

Uncle Gilbert leaned in. "Yes, there are different places that help the physically handicapped," he said. "You could talk to them about Jenny."

My face lit up, and the depression evaporated. I didn't know I could keep her, and I didn't know I could find places that would help her.

# CHAPTER TWELVE

In those days, a full-time babysitter cost twenty dollars a week, and I could find one in the Wichita Eagle and Beacon want ads. After I tried out various babysitters, I noticed an ad from an older lady who lived about two blocks from me. This was perfect. I gave her a call and pulled up to a small brick house.

Fern was a thin, soft-spoken, brown-haired retired lady who lived by herself in a two-bedroom, one-bath home. Her living room contained pictures of landscapes, comfy chairs, and a sofa with soft cushions of gold, reds, and greens. Long floral drapes hung to the floor, and a small piano with a bench tucked under it was topped with carefully arranged black and white family pictures. Her home smelled of scented soap, and the only sound was the ticking of the wooden wall clock.

Fern was taken in by Jenny's pretty face, light brown hair, green eyes, and sweet disposition.

"She doesn't sit up by herself, so you'll have to hold her head when you carry her." Fern was careful to place her hand under Jenny's head as I set her in Fern's open arms.

"That's fine." Fern's eyes sparkled as she looked down at her and started to play peekaboo.

"Would you like to give it a try in the morning?" Then I remembered. "Oh, how much do you charge?"

"Twenty-five dollars a week." Fern smiled down at Jenny and kept rocking her. My face fell, but I told her I'd drop her off in the morning.

♦ ♦ ♦

The next day, I picked her up from Fern's and carried Jenny, her diaper bag, and her yellow plastic carrier to the passenger side of my yellow Volkswagen. I put the diaper bag on the floor, laid the carrier in the passenger seat facing me, and situated Jenny in the carrier. After I planted myself in the driver's seat, I turned the key, looked over my shoulder, and backed my car out of the driveway. I looked down at Jenny and noticed that she started to wiggle and hold up her arms. She cooed and turned her head this way and that. She hadn't acted that way with any of the other babysitters.

As I started down the street, I glanced back down at Jenny and then up again and stared at the road. My mind started to add up the extra cost. Babysitting would cost as much as my rent—some months had five weeks, so it would be even more! I turned my head to her again and then back to the road scratching my neck. Jenny was still stirring and reaching out her hands. When I pulled up to the front of my apartment, I turned off the car and sauntered around to the passenger side. I took the blanket off Jenny and lifted her out of her plastic carrier.

"OK, Jenny," I said. "I'll pay the extra money."

◆ ◆ ◆

I continued to see Marlin, my lawyer, off and on, and one evening he suggested we meet downtown in a nightclub located on the top floor of a high-rise hotel. When the elevator opened, I entered a dimly lit room with walnut tables topped with candles and surrounded with comfortable black leather chairs. Low murmurings of conversation and soft laughter mingled with soothing instrumental music. Men in dark suits had unbuttoned the top button of their starched white shirts, so they could loosen the ties that had a chokehold on them. In the hand that had a gold band wrapped around their third finger, they held a small glass packed with ice cubes and amber-colored liquid. They laughed and flirted with the women who sat across from them, and their breath smelled of cigarette smoke and alcohol.

Marlin leaned back in a leather chair, held a scotch and water in one hand, and waved to me with the other. After I ordered a Tom Collins and lit a cigarette, we chitchatted back and forth about nothing. Seated at the bar behind us was a chatty, dark-haired woman. All of a sudden, she recognized Marlin.

"Marlin?" She paused and gazed at him with her head tilted to the side.

Marlin turned, and instantaneously, his eyes sparkled and a wide grin spread across his face. "Joanne!" Marlin stood up and hugged her. "Come join us," he said.

Marlin pointed back and forth to Joanne and then to me. "Joanne—Jackie—Jackie—Joanne."

I smiled and stuck out my hand. "Hello," I said.

"Hi!" She pumped my hand once, scooted in her chair close to Marlin, and leaned toward him with the corners of her mouth turned up. She waved her hands around with gusto as she talked about people they knew and tossed out jokes here and there. Marlin, obviously enthralled, sparkled and laughed as he occasionally gave her a good-natured shove.

I didn't say anything, but no one noticed. Before long, my chest started to ache, and I didn't know what to do. After an hour of this display of comradery, a flush crept across my face. Finally, I dug deep inside myself and mustered up the courage to stand up. I unwound my coat from the back of my chair and put it on as I marched toward the elevator.

When Marlin figured out what I was doing, he chased after me to the elevator. After I pushed the button for the first floor, I stood in the back of the elevator and faced Marlin as he held the door open with one arm and stretched his face toward me.

"I'll call you," he said. I just continued to stand there and stare at him until the elevator doors shut him out.

◆ ◆ ◆

When I turned sixteen, my parents told me I was now old enough to get a job, and from here on out, I had to buy my own clothes. So, in the summertime, I took a city bus from Waldo to downtown, and after I got off the bus, I walked down Main Street to the tiny Mode O'Day dress shop. Mode O'Day was always filled with wrinkled-faced ladies who smelled of cheap perfume. The ding of the bell every time the front door opened mingled with conversations and the sliding of hangers across racks of flowered dresses. Mrs. Brooks always had double the sales tickets of anyone else. She was a middle-aged African-American woman with a hearty laugh and friendly smile as she headed to the dressing room with an arm full of dresses. I can still see her tilt her head and nod at the reflection of a skeptical gray-haired lady standing in front of a mirror as tags hung from a yellow dress with splashes of dark pink. Her face immediately lit up when she heard Mrs. Brooks say, "That looks so smart on you!"

As for me, I couldn't see the difference between one flowered dress or another. Even though I always turned in the fewest sales tickets, it didn't matter because selling was not my primary job. At the end of the day, I took the stack of sales tickets, set them beside an adding machine, and punched in the amount that was written at the bottom of each ticket. Then, I had to count all the cash in the box and compare the numbers. If they didn't match, I had to keep searching, counting, and comparing until they were the same—to the penny.

Every week I would cash my check and walk to a store like Jones or Macy's and buy one or two upscale dresses that cost eighteen dollars each. The first time I showed off my new dress to my best friend, I watched her face and waited for her nod of approval. When I heard, "That's so cute" or "It looks great," I took a deep breath, pushed my shoulders back, and my chin lifted a little. For the first time in my life, I got a glimpse into what it felt like to be independent.

◆ ◆ ◆

Jenny had on clean, soft pink pajamas, her hair was combed and wet, and she smelled of Johnson and Johnson baby lotion. I held her close and fed her the last bottle of the night.

I had never been without a man, and for the first time in my life, I didn't feel the need for one—either financially or emotionally. I was *free*. I had a warm home, a kitchen cabinet full of baby food jars of fruit, vegetables, and meat along with cans of formula and a box of dry milk. I had a good job with insurance, and all the love I needed was right here.

For a month, Aunt Lee pestered me about going back to Dr. Robinson. I got tired of saying "no," and I knew Jenny needed a good pediatrician, so I finally succumbed.

This time, Aunt Lee wasn't with me when I sat in the small examination room waiting for Dr. Robinson. Since this was just a consultation, Jenny sat on my lap. I stared at the various diplomas on the wall and the cotton balls on the table. The aura of disinfectant was barely noticeable. After a while, Dr. Robinson came through the door dressed in the typical white lab coat, and a stethoscope hung around his neck. I shifted in my seat, but Dr. Robinson didn't allow for any uncomfortable silence.

"I'm not going to tell you that you need to put Jenny in an institution." He pulled up a chair and sat down directly in front of me.

He fixed his eyes on mine, and I got the impression that he wanted me to take heed of what he was about to say.

"I've seen mothers who have children like Jenny, and I've seen them devote their whole lives to caring for them." His eyes bore into mine. "When or if something happens to the child, they are left alone—and old." He paused as if to let that sink in.

"You are an attractive young lady," he said without a hint of a smile but as simply a matter of fact. "I know you want to take care of Jenny, but you also need to have a social life. You need to get out and not let your entire life be driven by caring for her."

When he was finished, he kept his eyes on me and waited. I fixated on his face and scrutinized his words. After a moment of silence, I told him I would do that—and I did.

# CHAPTER THIRTEEN

After I got settled into my job at Cessna and the holidays were over, I followed Aunt Francie's (Uncle Gilbert's wife) suggestion and found the phone number for Services for the Blind. When I saw the call had to be made to *Topeka*, I knew it would add several dollars to my phone bill. I sat on the edge of my bed, and before I lifted the receiver off the avocado green rotary desk phone, I rubbed the sweat off my hands and onto my jeans. I heard a click and a woman's voice say, "Kansas State Department for Services for the Blind." After a brief pause, I stammered and spewed out a concoction of mismatched words, but, eventually, she got the message. The gentleness in her voice helped my heart slow down, and the next day I called Dr. Robinson's office and the KU Medical Center Records Department in Kansas City. I asked both offices if they would send Jenny's medical records to the address the lady had given me.

A couple of weeks later, I drove home from Cessna, pulled up to my red brick duplex, and gathered Jenny and all her belongings out of the backseat. I managed to balance Jenny and all her stuff while I pulled my mail out of the tin mailbox that was bolted to the side of my front door, and I finagled the key into the keyhole. Once inside, I unloaded my arms and flipped through advertisements and a couple of medical bills before I saw a letter from the Educational Clinical Team and Review Board.

My whole face lit up as I read their response. They would "offer whatever support possible" to me during her preschool years. They went on to say that the Special Education Section "is processing a claim for paraprofessional funds in establishing a program for Jennifer," and my continuing contacts would be with Ed and Sandy. With a huge smile on my face, I lifted Jenny out of her carrier, held her close, and rocked her back and forth.

In no time at all, I'd found a paraprofessional who was willing to go to Fern's house and work with Jenny. My next step was to have Jenny evaluated by a physical therapist.

◆ ◆ ◆

Jenny was born at KU Medical Center, and I remembered when Jenny was about two months old, a thin, dark-skinned doctor with black-rimmed glasses told me he was from India, and he was in the U.S. studying at KU. He examined her thoroughly—more so than any of the others. Eventually, he mentioned something about a rubella titer.

"What's that?" I asked.

"It's when the mother has German measles during pregnancy." As far as I knew, I had never had German measles, and Tony said he hadn't either.

The doctor scrutinized every inch of Jenny and continued to gape at her as he absentmindedly commented, "She's an interesting baby. I wish I could be around to see what happens with her." My eyebrows drew together, and my head tilted, but I didn't think to ask why he said that.

Now, I wondered if the doctor with the black-rimmed glasses *knew* something was wrong with Jenny, and he was trying to figure out a reason for it. Whenever I asked Dr. Robinson what could be the reason for Jenny's brain damage, he just shrugged his shoulders and shook his head. "It's hard to know."

◆ ◆ ◆

To get Jenny's evaluation for physical therapy, I had to drive three hours from Wichita to Kansas City and go to an affiliate facility for pediatrics at KU. The floors of the facility were checkered with large, black and white tiles that smelled of floor wax. I laid Jenny on the plastic padded examination table topped with an ironed white sheet that gave off a slight scent of bleach. I took everything off Jenny except her diaper as directed by the white-uniformed nurse, who had just left. A short time later, the curly-headed physical therapist in a white lab coat stretched out her hand and introduced herself. She averted her eyes to Jenny, curved her hands around Jenny's chest, and lifted her to a vertical position as she scanned her physically. She smiled at Jenny and watched her eyes and how she responded when she stretched her face toward her and said, "Boo." She jerked back again with an open-mouthed grin and wide eyes with raised eyebrows.

The physical therapist knew how to play with Jenny in a way that meant something. She tested her gross motor skills by noting how well Jenny held her head, which she couldn't do well, and she pushed, stretched, and moved her legs and arms every which way. For her fine motor development, the therapist did things like shake a rattle toward her. It looked like play to me, but I learned that she was monitoring Jenny to see if she could hear where the rattling noise came from and if she would take it. If Jenny *did* take it, the therapist watched the clock to see how long she held it or if she transferred it to her other hand. She observed and recorded every response.

After an hour of testing, she wrote up a detailed plan of various exercises. After the paper was filled with drawings, she swung toward me. She glanced back and forth between me and the paper, pointed to each drawing, and clarified each movement. I kept asking questions, so she had to explain and re-explain everything. I knew I had to communicate all this to the paraprofessional, and I couldn't make a mistake. As I gathered Jenny and put things back into her diaper bag, I thanked her over and over again and scheduled her next appointment.

Even though it was April, the weather was cold and drizzly, but I didn't care. I covered Jenny's face and hurried to my yellow Volkswagen. I laid her in her yellow carrier in the back seat and tucked a blanket around her. After the car heated up and I was on the Kansas Turnpike, I lit up a cigarette and cracked my window. I peered into my rearview mirror and saw Jenny's closed eyes and heard her even breathing. Even though it was dark, cold, and rainy outside, a smile was still plastered on my face, and I turned up the radio and sang along with "Tie a Yellow Ribbon Round the Ole Oak Tree."

My paraprofessional, Phyllis, was a hyperactive woman in her middle thirties with shoulder-length, blond hair and a contagious grin. She flitted around my living room ready to take on any challenge that had to do with Jenny. We laid Jenny on a blanket on the living room floor, and after we maneuvered her limbs this way and that—according to the written instructions for gross motor skills—we proceeded to the exercises having to do with her fine motor development. We read, practiced, and read again until we were both confident that we had it right.

◆ ◆ ◆

The Institute of Logopedics in Wichita helped children with speech defects and other physical disabilities. When Jenny was a year old, I rolled her stroller through the front doors and down the hallway of the Institute of Logopedics. The place was filled with sounds of children's laughter and instructions from the mouths of jolly physical therapists and beaming teachers as they encouraged disabled children to walk from here to there or to put this string inside that hole of the tennis shoe. Smells of candy, crayons, and the cutting of construction paper rolled out of rooms that held children who were taught how to use scissors, paste this onto that, and show how close to the lines they could color.

I entered the Evaluation Unit and laid Jenny on the examination table. The no-nonsense examiner used things like different lights to check her eyesight and cracker pieces to check her chewing, sucking, and swallowing. After making note after note, she closed the folder and told me they would be in touch.

A week later, I opened a letter titled "Evaluation Unit Summary Report" and found that she is "essentially blind though there is response to light" and "All behavior and speech were at about the two to three-month level." I muttered a quiet "thank you" to God when I read that "auditory testing revealed hearing to be near normal limits."

I called Phyllis, and she said she would be happy to take Jenny to the Institute of Logopedics once a month for physical therapy and once a month for audiology.

Three months later, I pulled a letter from the tin mailbox beside my front door and noted that the return address was "University Affiliated Facilities for Pediatric Services and Training." The letter was from Sandy, my assigned contact, and she wrote that there was no record that Phyllis "was ever approved or hired." So, for right now, she guessed, Phyllis "will have to terminate unless you and she can work something out between you." Sandy added that she was "just sick about this."

# CHAPTER FOURTEEN

Eva Mae, my religious aunt who lived in California, was in Wichita for a week to help my grandmother, who was in the hospital. Eva Mae was shorter than her siblings, a bit plump, and she had a head full of dark hair, except for a white streak that came up out of nowhere. She was quick to joke, quick to laugh, and quick to talk about God.

On a cool, dark Saturday evening, I pulled in front of my grandmother's cozy red brick two-bedroom, one-bath home. I tapped on the front door, and Eva Mae gave me a wide, toothy grin as she unlatched the screen door and held it open. As soon as I stepped through the door, she reached over Jenny, threw her arms around my neck, and squeezed me. When Eva Mae let me go, she gave Jenny a quick tickle under her chin and trotted across cottony beige carpet toward the corner of the living room to a polished wood cabinet that held the TV. She bent and turned the volume knob to the left. "That's better," she said. When I saw the white socks that covered her feet, I kicked off my brown ankle boots and lined them up beside the door. The room smelled of furniture polish and baked dessert.

Eva Mae set a tall glass of sweetened iced tea on the table beside the creamed-colored sofa, handed me a freshly ironed white sheet, and returned to the kitchen to resume clanging dishes and rearranging knickknacks on the counter. I unfolded the sheet and got on my knees to smooth out wrinkles and straighten corners. I pulled Jenny out of her carrier, laid her on the sheet, and took off her light-blue and white striped T-shirt and light-blue corduroy overalls. After I changed her diaper, I pulled her arms through the sleeves of her soft yellow pajamas and snapped all the necessary snaps. I opened the diaper bag and took out a bottle that held Carnation's Instant Milk. After adding some warm water from the kitchen faucet, I mixed it by repeatedly turning the bottle upside down and back again as I traipsed back across the carpet and sat cross-legged on the white sheet. I pulled Jenny up on my lap, squeezed the nipple between her lips, and encouraged her to eat.

Eva Mae wrung out the dishcloth and hung up her apron before she returned to the living room with bright eyes and an excited grin. Jenny finally started sucking, so I leaned back against the bottom of the sofa, and my whole body decompressed.

After the usual social niceties such as "I'm doing fine," and "Your grandmother is doing well," and "Yes, I'll be here about a week," Eva Mae found a way to introduce her favorite subject: God, and she took off on a rampage.

Eva Mae didn't say much about God per se, but she talked a lot about Jesus. Jesus loves me; in fact, Jesus loves me so much that He died for me, and I needed to repent. Did I know I was a sinner? All of us must believe in Jesus, so we can go to heaven. Do I want to go to heaven? If I pray and ask Jesus into my heart, I will go to heaven.

"Would you like to pray right now and ask Jesus into your heart?" Her eyes bore into mine, and I knew this was intensely important to her.

"Yes," I said. I hadn't thought much about my sin, and I had no idea what the word *repent* meant, but Eva Mae said that I just needed to say this prayer. We both bowed our heads, and I followed her lead. I told God that I was a sinner, and I wanted Jesus to come into my heart.

When I raised my eyes, Aunt Eve's whole face gleamed, and she swiped her hands against each other a couple of times. "That's it!" A huge grin spread across her face, and her eyes sparkled. I smiled back and thought, *Jesus must be very important.* After I had gathered Jenny's things and headed toward the door, she mentioned something about the First Evangelical Free Church.

"It's really close to you, and they have people there who can explain things to you," she said. In confusion, I stared at her with a tilted head and eyebrows that squished together.

The most notable thing I learned from Eva Mae that night was that Jesus is extremely important, and I needed to pray to Him too. So, that night—and all the nights thereafter—I would lie in bed with my face to the ceiling, my eyes closed, and my fingers crisscrossed across my chest. I would whisper the entire Lord's Prayer, and after I said "amen" to that prayer, I would say another prayer—specifically to Jesus.

✦ ✦ ✦

Every weekday morning, I got up at 7:10, unrolled my long hair, smeared makeup on my face, brushed out my hair, and threw on a dress. I lifted Jenny out of her crib, put on her coat, grabbed her diaper bag, and dropped her off at Fern's at 7:25. After I parked my yellow Volkswagen in the Cessna parking lot, I sprinted through the parking lot and into the guard shack, snatched my timecard off the rack, and clocked in at exactly 7:30. Through the day, I assigned *N* numbers and figured out the weight and balance of airplanes. To do this, I snatched the folder for each aircraft from my inbox and flipped through the paperwork to find numbers that fit into a set formula. I placed the fingers on my left hand underneath those numbers and placed the fingers on my right hand on top of the adding machine on my desk. I glared at the number on top of my left-hand finger and blindly added and subtracted with my right hand until I knew the correct weight and balance of the aircraft. At the 10:00 morning break, I put change in the candy machine and pulled the lever for a Snickers bar, and then put money in the beverage machine and pulled the lever for Coke. I repeated that ritual for the 2:00 afternoon break, and I ate lunch in the cafeteria with Cathy and Annette.

At 4:30 in the afternoon, I left work, picked up Jenny, and began the evening ritual. For my dinner, I took out a frozen hamburger patty from the top freezer and plopped it in a frying pan. I spread Ketchup over two pieces of white sandwich bread, scooped out a handful of Lay's Potato Chips, and laid them beside my pseudo hamburger. After five minutes, I cleaned my plate and pan in a sink of soapy water and took down three baby food jars from the cabinet: fruit, vegetables, and meat. I set the jars of vegetables and meat in a pan of boiling water and poured milk into Jenny's bottle. I scooped out the warmed vegetables into one section of Jenny's pink floral baby plate, the warmed meat in the second section, and the fruit in the third section. After putting a little Ketchup on her meat, I set the plate on the dinette table alongside a green and white pack of Salem Lights cigarettes with a matchbook on top and pulled up one of the two chairs. After I lit a cigarette and blew smoke up and into the air, I set it in the glass ashtray. I snapped a plastic bib around Jenny's neck, leaned her back in the crook of my arm, and began the hour-long skirmish of getting food down her.

"That's a good girl!" I said after she took the first bite of vegetables and swallowed. "Let's try another." I scooped a bite of warmed meat into her mouth, but she wouldn't swallow. "Come on," I said with a sweet, prompting voice. I put my finger under her chin and rolled it around. She swallowed. "Yay! Good girl!" I went around her plate and got down one bite of each food item. By the second round, Jenny would start to turn her head this way and that. I tightened my grip around her and shoved another bite of food into her mouth. It lay there, but some of it spilled out, so I ran the spoon over her lips and stuffed it back in her mouth again. She started to fuss, but she swallowed it. "Good girl!" For the next couple of bites, I shoved food into her mouth and worked my finger under her chin and around her cheeks to mimic chewing motions and movements. I scooped food from around her mouth and, again, squished it back in. "Come on, you can do it," I repeated. She had not eaten more than a couple of bites from each food section of her plate, and I knew I had to get more food down her. She fussed and started to cry. I laid the spoon down, held her upright, and bounced her on my knee. After a couple of minutes, I said, "Let's try it again." As before, I cradled her head in my arm and scooped half of a teaspoon of meat with fruit on the end. When I placed it in her mouth, she started to cry again—but harder. Her face started to turn red, and she held her breath with some food in her mouth and some spilling out. When she gasped for air, she swallowed the food at the same time she breathed in. For a few more bites, I managed to get food down her, but I frowned and rubbed my eyebrow because she mainly swallowed when she cried and gasped for air. After about a third of her food was gone, I threw out the rest of the baby food and emptied my glass ashtray, which now held three cigarette butts. I carried her to the bathroom at the end of the hall, turned on the faucet, and regulated the water temperature for her bath. By 8:00, she was bathed, her hair was washed and combed, and she smelled like Johnson's Baby Shampoo and baby powder. I kissed her lips, cheeks, and neck and hugged her tight before I laid her in her white crib beside my bed, pulled up her blanket, and tucked it under her chin.

# CHAPTER FIFTEEN

Jane worked in the Engineering Department at Cessna, and about every two weeks or so, I'd call Fern to see if she could keep Jenny for an extra couple of hours. Jane had a tremendous amount of long, curly auburn hair that was as flighty as she was. She enhanced her green eyes by spreading earth-green eyeshadow across her lids and gluing on false eyelashes; she also magnified her full lips by applying glossy coral lipstick. She'd chuckle after each coarse joke or raunchy comment she made and then turn her head to see my reaction as I sat in the passenger seat of her 1969 red Ford Mustang. Jane leaned toward the radio, turned up the volume, and bellowed along to the words of "Brandy (You're a Fine Girl)" by Looking Glass. When she offered me marijuana, I just shook my head and lit up a cigarette. She lit a joint for herself and held the marijuana in one hand and a regular cigarette in the other. She tried to alternate taking a drag from the marijuana and then a drag from the cigarette, but she'd get them mixed up. "I can't ever remember which one I'm supposed to take a drag on next." Her eyes flicked from one hand to the other.

O'Brien's was a smoky local bar with lots of lively chatter in the background and glasses clanging behind the bar as the bartender soaped them up and swooshed them under hot water. We pulled out wooden chairs from under a shiny wood table, and I ordered a Tom Collins while Jane ordered a scotch and water. She called me her drinking buddy. After they set the drinks down in front of us, we lit cigarettes, and I mentioned that Jenny's medical bills were mounting.

She stopped smiling and gave me all her attention. "Why?"

"I have to take her to the doctor every time she gets sick—and she gets sick a lot." I picked up my Tom Collins, took a drink, and lifted my lipstick-coated cigarette from the ashtray and took a drag. I noticed that the guy at the next table was staring at Jane, but she didn't seem to notice.

"What do you mean she gets sick a lot?" She leaned in toward me, and her eyebrows drew together.

"She gets pneumonia a lot, so I have hospital bills too," I said.

Jane propped her elbow on the table and rested her hand under her chin. She stared off into nowhere and, absentmindedly, took a swallow of her scotch and water.

"You know waitresses at fine restaurants make a lot of money," she said. "You could make $30 to $40 a night."

My head jerked back, and my posture stiffened. "Really?"

"Sure," she said. "You could do that and still keep your job at Cessna."

Thinking out loud, I muttered, "Yeah. I could work on Friday and

Saturday nights, and I could make—let's see." I picked up a pen from the table and started scribbling numbers on a napkin. "That would be an extra $240 a month, but I'd still have to get a babysitter for Jenny."

"That's OK. It's probably the best-paying part-time job you'll find." She took another drink of scotch and water and turned her attention to the guy at the next table. After she gave him a smile and a wink, he and his friend were sitting at our table.

Two hours later, Jane dropped me off at my yellow Volkswagen in the Cessna parking lot. On my drive to Fern's, Dr. Robinson's words popped into my mind. *I could make extra money and have a social life at the same time.*

✦ ✦ ✦

Scotch and Sirloin was a small, but popular, fine-dining restaurant. The dark interior was interrupted only by soft candlelight on dark-wood tables and beams of light that came from underneath the polished walnut bar that curved around the center of the back wall. The one bartender, John, wore a plaid shirt with sleeves rolled up to his elbows and a white bar cloth slung over his shoulder. He was able to pour different kinds of alcohol into a shaker, wash glasses, and take orders all while throwing coins and cash into the metal register and scurrying from one end of the bar to the other with a smile on his face. Whiffs of smoked steak, alcohol, and cigarettes mingled throughout the restaurant along with murmurings of quiet conversations and occasional bursts of laughter. The owners were a husband-and-wife duo, and both were shrewd, kindhearted, and patient. When I first started, I was back in the kitchen, and the husband grabbed a steak out of the freezer and began to explain how he only bought high-quality steaks. He pointed to the frozen steak and moved his finger around various parts of the meat and marbled fat to show me what he was looking for. When he finished, he turned back to the freezer with his chest thrust out and a gleam in his eye. During a conversation with his wife about their popular French onion soup, she confided in me with a wink and a grin. "It's Lipton Dry Onion Soup."

By 5:00, the regulars were planted in their seats at the end of the bar and conversed with the bartender and waitresses until the restaurant started to fill up. By 7:00, there was no time for socializing.

In those days, waitresses had to take the drink order, deliver the drink order, take the appetizer order, deliver the appetizer order, take the salad order, deliver the salad order, take the entrée order, deliver the entrée order, take the dessert order, deliver the dessert order, collect the money, and deliver the change—all in an efficient, timely manner.

A proficient waitress delivered the drinks at one table while asking if they needed anything else; she then delivered French onion soup at the next table and took the salad order; she picked up the tab at the next table, and she took the entrée order at the last table and asked if they needed more drinks. She would then turn in the salad and entrée orders, and while the drink order was being filled, she would get change for the tab. After her tray was brimming with food and drinks, she hoisted it up, placed her flattened right hand with fingers spread apart under the center of the tray, and glided across hardwood floors.

I, on the other hand, would take a salad order from one table and turn it in. Then, I would go back and pick up glasses from one table and ask if they wanted more drinks. If they did, I'd turn in that drink order, and if they didn't, I would get their tab ready. It didn't take long before John would flag me over with a heavy sigh and narrow eyes.

"This is your drink order, and your entrée orders have been sitting on the counter for five minutes."

Customers would tap their feet, and when they caught my eye, they would motion to me with lifted hands before turning back to their friends and rolling their eyes. One time I picked up a flaming Grand Marnier from the bartender, and instead of putting it on a tray, I wrapped my fingers around the stem and walked, oh-so carefully, toward the table where it belonged. One—then two—flaming drops fell on my fingers. Within seconds, the glass flew down the walnut bar, and the bar became a sea of flames.

After a couple of months, John approached me one Saturday night after closing and said he needed to talk to me. He came out from behind the bar, scooted out a wooden chair from under a table for two, and pointed to the second chair for me. He cleared his throat and shifted in his chair before he spoke.

"The owners have told me that we need to let one of the waitresses go," he said. He wouldn't look at me as he rubbed the back of his neck.

"I know I'm not as good as the others, and I understand if you need to cut back." I bit my lips, and my chest started to squeeze in.

"Yeah," he said as he leaned toward me and put his elbows on the table. "They know you try. Look, Jackie—you are cute as a button, and

I hate to have to tell you this." John started to relax since the worst had been said.

"I really need the extra money." I felt tears starting to well up in my eyes, and I looked down at the floor.

John sat there for a moment studying my face. "Maybe you should try to just be a cocktail waitress." His head tilted slightly to the side, and he gave a half smile. "Then, you would only have to take drink orders."

We both stood up, and I gave him a hug. I dug through my purse for my keys, and I threw my coat over my arm. With drooped shoulders, I weaved between tables and out the door.

# CHAPTER SIXTEEN

Phyllis fought back tears when I broke the news that she was never approved or hired as a paraprofessional.

"What do you mean approved?" Phyllis gave me a blank look.

I lowered my voice and shrugged. "I really don't understand it all, but I guess the doctor was supposed to approve and hire you."

She stared down at her hands, and her voice broke. "It's OK." She knew I couldn't afford to pay her.

After we chattered on about nothing for several minutes, she said she would still take Jenny to her monthly appointments at the Institute of Logopedics, and she would only charge me a small fee. I jerked my head at the realization that I would need someone to do this, and I grasped her hand and hugged her.

Three months later, I pulled a letter from the tin mailbox by my door, opened the envelope, and slid out a thin carbon copy that read "Evaluation Unit Summary Report" at the top. They recommended, "that Jennifer be enrolled in an individual speech stimulation program at the Institute of Logopedics on a three-times a week basis and physical therapy three times a week." I held the letter to my chest and closed my eyes. *Thank you.* Then, I plopped down on the navy-flowered sofa, and my mind raced. *Phyllis won't be able to take her three times a week.*

That night, I lay on my back in bed, closed my eyes, and laced my fingers across my chest. After I said the Lord's Prayer and prayed to Jesus, I said, "God, please bring me someone who can take Jenny to those appointments."

◆ ◆ ◆

The next night, I tucked Jenny into bed, went back to my yellow Volkswagen, and grabbed a Wichita Eagle & Beacon from the front seat of my car. My supervisor at Cessna, Myrna, always gave me the daily paper, and most of the time the newspapers would just mount up in my car.

I sat down on the wooden chair at the dinette table and turned to the classifieds. I scanned the newspaper for phone numbers of babysitters who might be able to only work part-time and transport Jenny to the Institute of Logopedics. I took my list back to the bedroom, plopped down on the edge of my bed, and turned on the tall shaded lamp. I reached for the avocado-green receiver on the desk phone that sat on the end table that separated Jenny's crib and my double bed. I didn't stop dialing until I heard someone say, "That should work for me."

When I heard those words, my head shot up, and my voice jumped a little higher. "Really?" I fumbled for a pen to write down her name and number, and after we discussed times, days, and locations, I asked her how much she charged. Her answer made me cringe, but at this point, it didn't matter.

◆ ◆ ◆

One afternoon, I picked up the black receiver that sat on my desk at Cessna, and it was my new babysitter.

"Jenny's face is blue," she said.

My head jolted. "What?"

"I was driving home, and I noticed that her face looked kinda blue," she said.

I stood up, grabbed my coat that was draped over the back of my chair, and snatched my keys. I hurried toward the door and turned to my supervisor. "I'm meeting my babysitter at the hospital."

I pulled my yellow Volkswagen into a parking space in front of the emergency room entrance and sprinted through the front door and toward the woman behind the glass enclosure. I gasped for air and swallowed hard. "I'm Jennifer's mother." She led me through an inner door and pointed to her room. Jenny lay on an examination table surrounded by nurses and doctors. They all busied themselves as one put a mask over her face, another stuck a needle in her arm, and they all looked up at monitors. I leaned against the doorway and prayed in my mind. *Please, God. Let her be OK.* Within a few moments, the doctor came out.

"Jenny has pneumonia and will have to be admitted."

I blinked rapidly. "But why did she turn blue?"

"Lack of oxygen," he said. I tilted my head and bit my lip.

He glanced up from his notes and saw my furrowed eyebrows. "Sometimes the oxygen level goes down with pneumonia." With that, he swiveled around and sprinted out the door.

God answered my prayer—He always answered my prayers for Jenny.

◆ ◆ ◆

I applied for a job as a cocktail waitress at the Penthouse Club, and I got it. When I first entered the club, my heart raced, and I stammered when the waitress, who was assigned to me, tried to carry on a conversation. She gave me a sympathetic smile and an understanding nod.

The Penthouse had a windowed wall with glass to the ceiling, so before 5:00 p.m., the club was full of sunlight, and after 6:00 p.m., the picturesque window displayed a black sky and city lights. Soft black-leather chairs with low-rounded backs were placed symmetrically around low dark-wood tables, and the room was filled with serene instrumental music. The club smelled of perfume, cigarettes, and scotch. A glossy wood bar ran the length of a wall that stood in the middle of the club, and a couple of lawyers sat at the end of the bar on the same high-top stools they had been sitting on for years. In those days, there were no TVs plastered on the walls and no cell phones. Like every other bar, groups of businessmen sat in the soft, leather chairs around the low tables and jabbered with women they wanted to impress. People drank and conversed for hours, so cocktail waitresses kept busy.

During my first few days, I followed my assigned waitress as she strolled up to a table, smiled, and asked for the drink order. I noticed that she paid attention to the first person she asked. She wrote down the first drink order, moved to the next person and wrote down the second drink order, moved to the third person and wrote down the third drink order, and so on. When she laid the tab on the bar, the bartender took the tab, mixed all the drinks, clustered all the drinks together at the end of the bar, and laid her tab beside the drinks. She would set her tray on the bar, run her index finger down the tab, and place each drink on her tray in the exact order she had written on the tab. She lifted her tray, balanced it on her right hand with her fingers spread out underneath it, and held both her hand and her head high as she traipsed back to her table. All she had to do was remember whose drink was first and then make her way around the table. It didn't matter if there were two drink orders or ten; she placed the correct drink in front of the correct person. The next weekend, I had my own section. My shoulders were back, my chest was out, and my chin was high as I paraded around the club with my own tray filled with systematically placed drinks.

During that time, the liquor laws in Kansas were complicated. A person wasn't supposed to get an alcoholic drink unless they had a membership to the club. So, they had to join each club they wanted to buy a drink at. To get the membership, they had to wait ten days from the day of application to the day they could be served. That made it difficult for a club that sat on top of a hotel because guests of the hotel didn't *have* ten days. However, all clubs figured out a way to get around the law. All I knew was that I had to have the customers who stayed in the hotel fill out special bar tabs, and I had to collect money in a special way.

"Why do I have to do this?" they would inevitably ask.

"I don't know," I said as I set the drinks on the table. "Kansas has crazy laws, and you have to do it this way, or you can't drink alcohol here." They just took the pen from my hand and shook their heads as they scribbled on the tally card and handed it back to me.

Cocktail waitresses usually had to all dress alike. At the Penthouse Club, we wore long-sleeved minidresses that were silky black and topped with sprinkles of tiny gold stars. The flared A-lined skirt on the dress was so short I had to bend my knees and squat when setting drinks down on the low tables. I couldn't bend over—not even a little. All clubs stayed open until 3:00 a.m., so by the time we cleaned up and got out of there, I would knock on the door of my nighttime babysitter at 5:00 in the morning. If everyone went out to breakfast, it would be 6:00 a.m. Even though I got very little sleep, it was OK. I finally found a job I could do and have a social life at the same time.

# CHAPTER SEVENTEEN

To get to my office at Cessna, I had to enter the shop and traipse up metal stairs because offices were situated above the assembly line. I strode down a long hall with offices lined up on my right, and at the far end of the hall was the Quality Assurance Department—which was my office. There were four desks, and my desk sat next to the window that overlooked the assembly line. Maxine's desk was to the left of mine, Myrna's desk was to the left of hers, and my supervisor, John, sat behind me. Metal files were at the back of the office, and we all faced the door that led into the hallway.

The office had lots of fluorescent light, and each of the desks held a black rotary desk phone, typewriter, adding machine, inbox, and papers. The papers on Maxine's and Myrna's desks were paperclipped together and placed just so, the papers on John's desk were scattered here and there, and the papers on my desk were a mixture. The room smelled of typewriter ribbon, fresh paper, and cigarette smoke that hovered around the ashtray on my desk. The office sounded of tapping on typewriter keys, clicking on adding machines, and an occasional bing on the window next to me when some guy on the assembly line below threw a rivet at the window beside my desk.

Except for me, everyone in my office was old. John was probably in his sixties, and Maxine and Myrna were probably in their fifties. Both Myrna and Maxine went to the beauty parlor once a week to have their gray hair shampooed and set. Both wore wirerimmed glasses, and both pulled out salads and sandwiches when lunchtime rolled around. The only real difference was that Myrna was taller, thinner, and wore solid-colored dresses, while Maxine was shorter, plumper, and wore printed dresses. I noticed that Maxine would stare at the candy bar I brought back from the vending machine twice a day. Both ladies always spoke kind words to me and always asked about Jenny.

Within a few weeks of working Friday and Saturday nights at the Penthouse Club, I was asked to work on a particular Saturday morning at Cessna—and I agreed. I arranged to leave Jenny at her nighttime babysitter's house until noon that Saturday, so after leaving the club, I drove the thirty minutes home, changed, and sat at my desk at Cessna by the time the clock said 7:00 a.m. By 10:30 a.m., I was fast asleep in the bathroom stall as I rested my head against the wall.

At 11:00 a.m., I was jarred awake in the bathroom and disoriented for a moment. I stood, washed my hands, and as I inched down the long hallway, I glanced at a clock in one of the offices. I gasped when I realized I had been gone for almost thirty minutes! Back in my office, John's desk was empty, and Maxine and Myrna glared at my empty desk and then at each other shaking their heads and frowning. My pulse throbbed in my ears, and I could feel sweat accumulating on my forehead.

I ducked into the office, sat at my desk, and my fingers trembled when I picked up papers. When I glanced at Myrna and Maxine, it was the first time they did not return my smile. My mind ran wild. *I can't lose my job and my health insurance.*

Myrna said she had to make copies, and she stepped out of the office without making eye contact. Maxine continued to shuffle papers and didn't say a word.

I swallowed hard. "Maxine?"

Maxine looked up with a pinched expression and narrow eyes. A few moments passed by, and I realized she wasn't going to say anything.

"I fell asleep in the bathroom," I said. "I started working another job on the weekends a few weeks back, and I didn't get home until really late." A red flush crept across my face, and I cleared my throat.

Maxine went completely still. It was as if her mind was spiraling, and she was putting puzzle pieces together. Myrna and Maxine knew Jenny had been in and out of the hospital. In a few seconds, her facial muscles slacked, and she gave me a sad smile.

I had seen that same expression on other people's faces, too. I was confused as to why people pitied me. Jenny didn't know anything was wrong with her; she wasn't hurting or unhappy, and I was happier than I'd ever been in my life. Myrna and Maxine never said another word about it.

◆ ◆ ◆

I quit my job at the Penthouse Club because I got a job at the Rafters, which was about five minutes from my apartment. The only difference was that the Rafters was noisier and had boat oars and fish nets draped across the walls. I wore a sailor top with a white square collar outlined with navy-blue stripes and navy-blue short shorts. For the first couple of weeks, I put on the matching sailor hat and tipped it to the side, but I quit wearing it when I noticed the indentions it made in my long hair by the end of the night.

I watched as men would come into the bar with their mistresses, but at other times, they would come in with their wives. Men sat next to their wives and said nothing while their wives flipped ashes into ashtrays and giggled with upturned faces. A few days later, the same men would laugh, joke, and beam at their mistresses. I just shook my head and remembered when I was the wife who sat at home while my husband was out till all hours of the night. It seemed reasonable that if men could live this way, why couldn't I? I sure didn't want to get married, and I remembered my promise to Dr. Robinson.

I had to figure out how to have a social life without taking even more time away from Jenny. Since I got off work at the Rafters at 3:00 in the morning, I could go to breakfast and pick up Jenny at 6:00. During the week, I had to make time after I fed, bathed, and tucked her in bed. Therefore, if a guy was interested, we could go out to breakfast after work on the weekends, or he could knock on my door after 8:00 p.m. on a weekday. A couple of times a month, I would ask Fern to watch Jenny for a few extra hours if I wanted to go out on an actual date.

◆ ◆ ◆

Paula would frequently come into the Rafters, and we became quasi-friends. She had a rather plain face and somewhat long, stringy-brown hair, but she laughed a lot, and she knew how to attract rich, powerful men. She didn't care if they were married or single—as long as they had money and were successful. One evening, I had Fern keep Jenny for an extra three hours, and Paula and I pulled into the parking lot of a popular bar. Warm lighting and smoke filled the room along with the familiar sounds of glasses clanging and loud conversations mixed with the smell of cigarettes and alcohol. All of this made the place comfortable and inviting. We pulled out heavy wooden chairs from underneath a solid wooden table for four and settled in. Paula ordered a scotch and water, I ordered a Tom Collins, and both of us lit up cigarettes. Before long, she spotted the guy she was dating and waved to him as he stepped through the front door. I turned and watched a heavyset, dark-haired man jerk his head up in acknowledgment then lean his head toward the shorter man next to him and point toward us. Both men wore dark suits and held their heads high as they walked with wide steps toward our table. The taller guy was the rich client of the shorter guy, who was his high-powered lawyer. The rich client greeted Paula with a swift hug and gave me a quick handshake.

The rich client introduced himself and his high-powered lawyer, who grinned and nodded at me and pulled up the last chair. Paula introduced me, and both guys settled back with awkward smiles plastered on their faces. The lawyer was eleven years older than I was, had thinning hair, and wore wire-framed glasses. Both men ordered scotch and water, and both men were married with kids.

After an hour of drinking, our table for dinner was ready, so we all strolled to the back and sat at a candlelit table covered with a white tablecloth and white cloth napkins. Everyone ordered steak and lobster, and by this time, everyone's guard was down. The lawyer cracked jokes and made comments that made me laugh, but Paula and the rich client would only offer either an obligatory chuckle or just look at each other and shake their heads and roll their eyes.

I took a drag off my cigarette. "What's your wife like?" I sat back in my chair with my arms folded across my chest.

"She's great," he said. "A really good woman and a good mom." He took a drink and smiled at me. The high-powered lawyer guy took my number, and for the next two years—depending on my dating situation—he would drift in and out of my life.

# CHAPTER EIGHTEEN

I laid Jenny in her warm bath. When the warm water circled half her face and surrounded her body, her lips would turn into a grin. She would move her legs and arms as I soaped up her washcloth. I lifted the back of her head and began spreading Ivory soap around her face, ears, and down to her toes. I laid her back into the water and rinsed her off, and that's when I noticed it. Her eyes rolled up, just a tad, and her hands and arms stiffened and shook—oh so slightly. I finished rinsing off all the soap, wrung out the washcloth, and set it on the side of the tub. I flipped the drain release and immediately suctioned water gurgled then swirled around the drain. I laid a clean towel down beside the tub and lifted Jenny out of the bathtub and onto the towel, and with another clean towel, I rubbed her hair, face, tummy, legs, and feet. I wrapped the towel around her, lifted her off the floor, and balanced her on my hip as I dabbed toothpaste on her toothbrush, and I sat on the lid of the stool. After I arranged Jenny on my lap, I maneuvered the toothbrush into her mouth so I could brush the front and back of each of her tiny teeth. She was now clean inside and out, so I carried her into the bedroom and laid her on my bed to finish the nightly routine of sprinkling powder here and rubbing lotion there, diapering, combing hair, and pulling arms and legs through pajama holes. I stuck the end of her sippy cup between her lips, but she only took a little water. I kissed her lips, neck, and cheeks, and tucked her blanket around her.

I started paying attention and noticed that the eye-rolling and slight hand stiffening and shaking could happen at any time: when she ate, when she lay in her yellow carrier, or when I was just carrying her around. I picked up the receiver and dialed Dr. Robinson's office.

When I stepped through the doorway of Dr. Robinson's office, my hands were filled with the diaper bag, Jenny, and my purse. As soon as the short-haired receptionist saw me, she jumped up and guided me to a room in the back that was isolated from the germs of kids and moms in the waiting room. I sat in a discarded chair in a small room that held some old metal filing cabinets and an unused empty desk. I could hear banging and toddler talk as children played in the nearby waiting room along with a mother's high-pitched voice when she asked the receptionist how much longer she would have to wait. I glimpsed out the one window and noticed the white blossoms of a nearby dogwood tree swaying in the sunlight, and in my mind, I could smell spring. When it was Jenny's turn, the white-uniformed nurse peeked into my room and led me to the examination room. "How old is Jenny now?" she asked. She waved to my assigned room, and I set down the diaper bag and purse and laid Jenny on the examination table. "She's almost two."

"Hard to believe," she said with upturned lips. She looked down at Jenny. "Such a pretty dress!" she cooed as she bent down closer to Jenny's face. She looked back at me and placed her hand on the doorknob. "Just have a seat, and Dr. Robinson will be in shortly."

Dr. Robinson gave me a warm welcome as soon as he came through the doorway. Within a few moments, I told him how Jenny's eyes would roll back, and her arms and hands would stiffen—just a little—and shake—just a little. He picked up his clipboard and a pen to write down my answers to the questions he was about to ask.

"How long have you been noticing this?"

"Oh, maybe a couple of weeks."

"How long would you say it lasts?"

"Oh, gosh. I didn't think to time it. Just a few seconds."

Dr. Robinson wrote on the clipboard, and when he was finished, he stood up and stepped toward the examination table. He listened to her chest and back and looked into her ears and eyes.

"Jenny is having grand mal seizures," he said as he wrapped the stethoscope around his neck and sat back down to record more information.

My mouth fell open, and I froze. After a few seconds, my voice shook, and I could only get out, "What? What did you say?"

Dr. Robinson glanced at me, and his head jarred when he saw my face. He laid down his clipboard and made eye contact with me. "Grand mal seizures are caused by abnormal electrical activity in the brain, so we can assume Jenny's seizures are probably a result of her brain damage. I'll write her a prescription for phenobarbital and Dilantin to help control them."

Dr. Robinson didn't seem all that concerned about them. *They must not be that bad,* I thought. He concentrated on his notes and writing out the prescriptions. With a polite grin, he handed me two small sheets of paper signed with an illegible signature. "Just give me a call if they get worse." With that, he turned and strutted out the door.

◆ ◆ ◆

Jenny sucked the Dilantin out of the spoon with ease, but when I gave her the phenobarbital, her forehead puckered, and she scrunched up her face as it turned red. Eventually, I was able to get the phenobarbital in pill form, so I could crush it and mix it with applesauce. Much better.

Three months later, I received a letter from the Institute of Logopedics telling me that Dr. Marsh had examined her, and Jenny had not made any progress during the summer months after she turned two, so he "did not believe that further physical therapy was indicated until the medicine and seizures were controlled or balanced out."

◆ ◆ ◆

Periodically, the Rafters would hire entertainers on Friday and Saturday nights. Usually, the entertainers were three or four guys who played instruments, sang, and told jokes. Once, they hired a twenty-six-year-old, harmonica-playing entertainer with dark hair and blue eyes. For a month, every Friday and Saturday night, he would stand on a makeshift stage, and a group of his friends would sit off to the side at a table for six. They drank Coke, clapped along with the music, and roared at his jokes. He and his friends seemed different, but I didn't know why. Their clothes and physical features were somewhat plain, but they always laughed, and they always had something nice to say.

A couple of times, the harmonica guy would join the rest of us for breakfast after we left the club at three thirty in the morning. When we all clamored through the door of the pancake house, the climate changed from quiet and empty to boisterous and chaotic. The waitress on duty was always happy to see us because we all had pockets of cash, and each of us knew the importance of tipping well. The well-lit restaurant contained red vinyl chairs tucked under Formica tables and smelled of bacon and eggs. I sat at the opposite end of the long table from the harmonica guy. His Coke-drinking friends had left the club long ago, but he wanted to tag along after work. Out of curiosity, I watched him nod his head and grin at the people who sat around him, and every once in a while, I'd hear him say something like, "I hear ya." To me, it sounded like a weak effort to fit in. For the past couple of weeks, I had smiled at him, teased him, and watched him, but he only responded with a polite grin before he turned his attention to his friends and his harmonica.

The next weekend, I stood at the end of the bar, and, for once, I wasn't busy. The harmonica guy sauntered up to the bar and stood beside me. I decided to give it another try, so I turned to him and chitchatted, and—for some reason—the subject of drugs came up out of nowhere.

"Do you take drugs?" I asked.

He hem-hawed around and gave me a nervous smile. "Uh, I used to, but I don't anymore."

I lit a cigarette, put it in the ashtray, and blew smoke out of the corner of my mouth and up into the air. He wiped his forehead, and his fingers seemed to tremble.

"Why did you quit?" I asked.

His face grimaced, and he started biting at his lips. It seemed to take everything he had inside of him to answer that question. He would not look at me, but he stared straight ahead. "I became a Christian."

I watched him continue to look into nothing, but his body started to lose its stiffness, and he lowered his head in relief. He turned to me and gave me a benign smile before he marched toward the stage.

I had no idea what he meant or why this was such a big deal. However, there was one thing I *did* know. I *did* know that he would *never* date me.

# CHAPTER NINETEEN

I worked every other Sunday night at the Rafters until 1:00 in the morning. In the fall when Jenny was two, she had an appointment in Kansas City for 8:00 Monday morning at KU Medical Center. After I got off work Sunday night, I pulled my yellow Volkswagen up to Jenny's nighttime babysitter's house at 1:30 a.m. I scooted my suitcase to the other side of the backseat and sat Jenny in her yellow carrier. I tucked a blanket all around her, climbed into the driver's seat, and lit a cigarette. When I turned onto the Kansas Turnpike, I cranked down my window and grabbed the ticket. I figured I would be at Vicki's at 5:00, which would give me—maybe—an hour's sleep before I had to get up, get dressed, get Jenny taken care of, and be at KU by 8:00. I turned the windshield wipers on and off according to the amount of light rain that splattered on the windshield.

About an hour and a half into the drive, the car jerked. I ignored it and turned up the radio, but the car wouldn't let me shrug off the problem for long. When I flew by the sign for Emporia, I turned off the radio, put both hands on the steering wheel, and leaned forward glued to the white lines in the center of the road that raced by. Within a few minutes, the car coughed and sputtered. I put my foot down harder on the accelerator, but the yellow Volkswagen wouldn't go any faster. The white lines slowed down, and finally, I had to pull over because my car wouldn't go over ten miles an hour. In disgust, I threw my head back and gazed at the ceiling of the car. Then, I glanced at the clock on the dash—it was 3:00 a.m. With a scowl on my face, I opened the car door and stepped out onto the black, wet asphalt. In the distance, I saw two headlights getting larger and larger. I stood in front of my car and started waving my arms over my head. The semi-trailer truck approached me at full speed and swept by me just as fast. The gust of wind it created made me stumble backward. I straightened up, pulled my shoulders back, and tried it again—and again. No one would stop. Eventually, the smirk on my face disappeared, and my arms fell lifeless by my side. My body started to tremble, and my stomach clenched. I trudged back to the car, opened the driver's door, and dropped into the driver's seat. It was fifty degrees outside, so I slammed the door on the chilly black night. A vacant look covered my face as I stared off into space. There was absolutely nothing I could do. Without moving a muscle, my eyelids slowly came down over my eyes, and I prayed to God for help.

A few moments later, I lifted my eyelids and saw the red taillights of a car that had just pulled over in front of me. A thirtysomething-year-old man with light brown hair opened his driver's seat door and smiled as he strode toward my car. I rolled down my window.

"Do you think your car can make it a mile?" He turned and pointed up the highway. "There's a gas station just up the road."

My voice shook. "I don't know, but I don't think so."

He stood silent for a moment. Then he looked down the road and back at me, and then at Jenny sleeping in the backseat. "Just follow me," he said. "If you can't make it, we'll figure something out."

◆ ◆ ◆

Five minutes later, I pulled up behind him into the gas station. Gas stations had attendants in those days, so he talked to the shop guy, who knew all about mechanics, and he waved goodbye to me and disappeared into the night.

The shop guy allowed Jenny and me to settle into his warm little shop that smelled of oil and gas. New tires were stacked beside the shop area, and a red circled Coca-Cola sign with white cursive lettering hung on the wall beside a candy vending machine that held Good & Plenty, Milk Duds, and Junior Mints. The other vending machine had a built-in cap opener and held several bottles of soda. The shop guy sat at an old wooden desk full of invoices and grease.

"Your fuel system is shot," he said. I stared at him. "It won't run anymore, and I can't fix it." He looked at me and Jenny.

"Do you, by any chance, have a car I can borrow?" I asked as I wrung my hands. "I'll be sure and get it back to you." I'm sure my face was full of innocence and desperation.

The shop guy looked outside at a possible car I could use and then back at me. His fingers tapped on the table, and his eyes blinked. "Be sure you bring it back," he said.

I thanked him over and over again as I loaded the suitcase and Jenny in the backseat of the white 1967 Ford Fairlane, and I drove back onto the Kansas Turnpike and headed east.

◆ ◆ ◆

When I laid Jenny in her yellow carrier during her evaluation, the brown-headed therapist looked at her legs stretched out beyond the end of the carrier, and told me that my insurance would probably cover a travel chair.

"A travel chair?" I asked. She showed me how the special-made chair would support her head and body, and with a quick flip of a side switch, the back legs would come up, so I could use it as a car seat too. My eyes widened in disbelief, and my heart jumped. She said she'd have the doctor send me a prescription by the end of the week.

My next stop was the dietitian. She was concerned about Jenny's weight. "She won't eat very much," I said. "I spend at least an hour a meal trying to get more food down her."

The dietitian just looked down at her notes and wrote out what she thought Jenny needed in order to gain weight. I told her Jenny would not eat that much, and her suggestions were impossible. Nevertheless, a month later she sent me a letter that said, "Jackie, this is a lot of food and is included to allow for growth. By all means gradually work up to these levels. Maybe try half this amount now and see how she gains weight." I guess it made her feel better to write out the impossible.

After I left Kansas City and headed west on the turnpike toward Wichita, I didn't allow my eyes to turn to the Emporia exit, but I kept driving the white 1967 Ford Fairlane past the shop guy's gas station and into Wichita.

❖ ❖ ❖

The high-power lawyer wanted me to go with him on an overnight trip to Dallas. His rich client and his current girlfriend would also be going. Paula was long gone. I made arrangements for Jenny, and we all climbed on the plane and headed for Dallas.

We ate, drank, and laughed, and the next morning, we caught an early flight back to Wichita. The wind made my hair fly every which way as we climbed up the stairs and stepped onto the plane. Before we had stumbled too far down the aisle, the lawyer pointed to my seat near the window and then pointed to the aisle seat for his rich client's tall, dark-haired girlfriend. After she and I sat down, he and his rich client kept walking down the aisle until they reached the back of the plane.

People with forced smiles clamored down the aisle and stuffed suitcases in overhead bins while they muttered an occasional "I'm sorry" and "Excuse me." It was early morning, so men wore suits and smelled of Brut aftershave, women wore dresses and smelled of hairspray, and both smelled of Wrigley's Spearmint gum. After everyone had buckled their seatbelts and the beautiful red-lipped airline stewardess had given the spiel on airline safety, the plane finally took off. As soon as the seatbelt sign and the no smoking sign dinged off, everyone reached for a cigarette and popped open the ashtray that was buried in the armrest.

The meek, dark-haired girlfriend, who sat beside me, had a plain face and a closed mouth. I laid my head back on the headrest and gazed out the window. For some reason, my conscience didn't seem to hurt with the other guys I dated, but it sure did with this lawyer. After a while, I turned to her with a pained expression.

"Does your conscience ever hurt?" I asked. Her head jolted, and she turned to me and scrutinized my face.

"I don't know," she said. She straightened her skirt and scratched at her cheek and neck. "I don't think about it that much. I mean—I love him, and I guess it's just the way it is."

"You *love* him?" I asked with raised eyebrows. When she saw my expression, she just shook her head and turned away.

I opened my mouth to say something but shut it again and gazed back over the clouds. *That's crazy to feel that way about a married man,* I thought. Her conscience might not have hurt, but mine sure did—for about two months.

# CHAPTER TWENTY

After working at the Rafters, I picked up Jenny by 6:00 a.m., changed her diaper, and tried to get some milk down her before I put her in her crib and slept for four—maybe five—hours. At 11:00, I fed, bathed, and dressed Jenny. Then, I took a bath, washed and rolled my hair, scrubbed the bathroom and kitchen, mopped and vacuumed floors, ran a cloth over all the furniture, and gathered all the dirty clothes. I wrapped a scarf around my jumbo rollers and propped Jenny on the laundromat table while I folded clothes and stacked them in the basket.

When Jenny was in the hospital, I skipped the cleaning and laundry and went directly to the hospital with my rollers wrapped in a scarf. Anytime I saw Jenny's chest cave in when she breathed, and she had a fever, I knew she probably had pneumonia and would be admitted to the hospital.

Jenny's hospital room was normally buzzing with the sound of oxygen flowing into the tent where she lay and conversations with white-uniformed nurses who came in and out asking me questions. The room smelled of medicine and bleach, but it still felt homey and relaxed rather than cold and sterile. Most of the time, I sat in the brown-padded chair beside Jenny's bed and rocked her, fed her, and jabbered with the nurses.

"Jenny eats so much better for you," said one nurse with a smile.

"Really?" I said with an incredulous stare. "Do you think she knows me?"

"Oh yeah—for sure." The corners of her mouth turned up as she watched Jenny. "None of us can get her to eat the way she eats for you." Her eyes went from Jenny to me, and I'm sure my eyes widened as I fixated on what she had just said. She winked at me and squeezed my shoulder before she strolled out the door.

Jenny didn't cough, so, periodically, nurses would bring in a suction machine, attach a size seven French catheter, and weave it down her nose. Then, they would gently draw it back up, sucking out phlegm from the back of her throat and through her nose.

"I wonder if I could get one of those," I said. "I mean, it would be great if I had one and could suction her at home."

She turned off the machine and wiped alcohol pads all over it. "I don't see why not," she said.

I asked Dr. Robinson, and he gave me a prescription for the suction machine. Now, whenever she needed it, I weaved the tube down Jenny's nose and throat and listened to the sound of phlegm gurgling out of her and through the tube. Her face would scrunch up—but only for a moment.

◆ ◆ ◆

A few weeks later, I pulled up to Fern's house in my 1972 brown Ford Torino. The shop guy had hunted me down and drove to Wichita to pick up his white Ford Fairlane. Luckily, my cousin owned a car dealership and got me financed for the Ford Torino.

I entered Fern's comfy house that smelled of flowers and baked cookies, and the living room illuminated as rays of sunshine streamed through her picture window. She asked me to stay a minute. I picked up Jenny, sank into Fern's cushiony sofa, and bounced her on my knee. When I glanced up at Fern, she seemed jumpy and wouldn't look at me.

"I'm getting nervous about Jenny," she said.

"Really? Why?" I no longer concentrated on Jenny but gave Fern my full attention.

"She gets sick, and I worry about her." Fern wrung her hands and paced back and forth across the living room carpet. "I'm thinking that maybe you should try to find someone else to watch her." Fern sat down in a nearby chair, but she sat up straight with her foot tapping the floor.

My heart stopped. When it started beating again, I tossed out every objection I could think of. I said things like "It will be okay" and "Jenny is so comfortable here."

Fern fiddled with her jewelry, tilted her head, and paused. "I just can't do it," she said. "I'm scared she will die." Fern stood up again and began pacing the floor.

I didn't want this to be happening, so I stayed on the couch rubbing my face and bouncing Jenny rapidly on my lap. Eventually, my shoulders slumped, and in a monotone voice, I said. "OK. I'll start looking for someone else."

Fern let out a huge breath and sat back down in the chair, but this time she fell back in relief. I sighed and stopped talking. I stood up and gathered Jenny's things. "See you tomorrow," I said as I trudged toward my Ford Torino.

Every night after that, I prayed for a babysitter. God had *always* provided a babysitter for Jenny—but this time He didn't.

◆ ◆ ◆

I dated various guys, but most of the time, the relationship ended within a couple of months. Aunt Lee once said, "You've sure done a lousy job of choosing men, but this time, Jenny does the screening for you." She was right. I had plenty of dates, but no one was interested in getting serious—and I didn't care.

For a couple of months, I dated the Italian owner of a popular restaurant. He had dark hair, dark eyes, and dark skin. He was a bit overweight and had a hearty laugh. Once, he told me, "No one wants to see a skinny owner of an Italian restaurant." His restaurant closed at 1:00 a.m., so he drove to the Rafters on weekends and sat at the end of the bar and drank scotch and water until closing time.

When we started dating, he took me to his restaurant for dinner. The quaint restaurant smelled of oregano and basil and was filled with tables covered with white tablecloths and topped with small candles. The sounds of Frank Sinatra music intermingled with the chatter of customers and the clamor of pans in the kitchen. When he introduced me to his regular patrons, I noticed that gray-haired ladies and balding men would sit up a little straighter when they heard him say their names.

Then—out of nowhere—he quit calling. He still sat at the end of the bar drinking scotch and water after his restaurant closed, but he didn't pay much attention to me. I'd stand by him, ask him questions with glossy eyes, and give him a quick touch, but he wouldn't respond. Eventually, I just shrugged my shoulders and strutted off. One night when I did this, I heard him yell at me across the restaurant.

"You know, I used to think people looked at me and thought, *That's sure a hot girl he's with*," he said.

I swallowed hard and turned to him. "What?"

Again, he bellowed across the restaurant. "I said I used to think people who saw me with you thought I was with a hot girl." The Italian guy's nostrils flared. All heads turned, and all eyes were on us. "They didn't think that, though," he continued. "They thought, *Why is he dating that slut*?" A smirk crossed his face, and he picked up his drink.

My face burned, and my heart pounded. *Is that what people think of me?* I raced to the bathroom and buried my face in my hands. A few minutes later, I took my hands off my face and stared at my reflection in the bathroom mirror. I straightened my makeup and hair, turned, and marched out as if nothing had happened.

# CHAPTER TWENTY-ONE

Jenny started running a fever, and Dr. Robinson was out of town. After flipping through the Yellow Pages, I found a pediatrician across town who said he could see her. I strapped Jenny into her state-of-the-art travel chair and wheeled her to the backseat of my Ford Torino. With a flip of a switch, the travel chair became a car seat.

I strolled Jenny into the blond-brick building, up the elevator to the second floor, and into the first room. A bouquet of roses sat on the counter in front of the glass that hid the dark-haired receptionist. The room smelled of clean carpet and scrubbed toys. Without looking up, she asked for my name, Jenny's name, and my insurance card. She handed me a brown clipboard with a pen attached, and I laid my purse on top of a *Parents' Magazine* on the end table and sat in a dark blue, cushioned chair. The only other mom in the waiting room flipped through a *Good Housekeeping* magazine as her baby slept in a white plastic carrier situated on the seat next to her. The only sounds came from papers flipping and pens scratching. When I handed back the completed forms, the dark-haired lady gave me a forced smile.

A white-uniformed nurse led me into a small room and pointed to the examination table covered with a white sheet. She wrote, and I explained. "Jenny has a fever, and she gets pneumonia frequently, so I think she needs an antibiotic." I undressed Jenny, folded her clothes, and lined up her shoes on the chair next to the examination table. The nurse finished writing and said the doctor would be in shortly. The usual framed doctoral degrees were nailed to the wall alongside wall-mounted medical gadgets. The room smelled of soap and medicine.

The new doctor was heavy, balding, and no-nonsense. He took Jenny's temperature, pushed the stethoscope against her chest, put a light in her ears, nose, and mouth, and laid her back gently onto the examination table. When he wrapped the stethoscope around his neck and headed toward the round swivel chair, I stepped up to the table and covered her with a blanket. He sat down and rested his arm on the counter with his pen ready to write.

"What do you think is wrong with Jenny?" he said. He gazed at me with sudden focus. He seemed more interested in what I thought than Jenny's pneumonia. My head flinched back slightly.

"She's profoundly brain damaged." I gave him a blank look.

"What does that mean—*exactly*?" He leaned back in his chair, crossed his arms, and observed my reaction.

I quit looking at him and cleared my throat. "It—it means that she will probably never walk, and—and she'll probably always need special care."

The doctor tilted his head to the side and hesitated. "How long?"

"How long what?"

"You said Jenny would probably always need special care. How long do you *think* she'll need special care?" The doctor scooted his swivel chair closer to me, rested both arms on his legs, and laced his fingers together. I stared down at him with my lips pressed together in a slight grimace. I glanced at Jenny and back to him.

"I—I don't know," I said. I felt restless, but there was nowhere to pace. The doctor stood up and turned back to the counter that held the folder and his papers. He didn't look at me.

"You know, children like this don't normally live more than five or six years." I no longer wanted to pace. My body froze, and my eyes began to blink rapidly. I couldn't talk.

When the doctor didn't hear a response, he turned and saw my ashen face, and with sudden focus, he tilted his head and said, "Have you never been told that before?"

I just barely shook my head. "No—no, I haven't."

His face reddened, and he crammed the papers into the folder on the counter and scratched out a prescription. "Someone should have told you." He laid the prescription on the counter and strode out. After he left, I slipped Jenny's dress over her head and put on her socks and shoes. My fingers shook when I picked up the prescription off the counter, and I rushed out.

◆ ◆ ◆

I raced to the car and positioned Jenny in the backseat. I flopped down in the driver's seat and sat in silence as I let the reality of the doctor's words wash over me. I pressed my forehead on the back of my two hands that were curled around the steering wheel and sobbed uncontrollably. I lost track of time. Eventually, my mind started to operate. I looked up and out the windshield. With all the sins in my life, I had never bothered to pray specifically for myself, and I didn't now. However, I remembered that God always answered my prayers for Jenny. A new determination rose within me. *I would not give up. I would fight for Jenny's life.* I whisked my palms across both my cheeks and the tears were gone. I turned the key, looked over my right shoulder, and backed out of the parking lot.

# CHAPTER TWENTY-TWO

My reputation was shot, and Fern kept asking me if I'd found another babysitter. I had been divorced for going on three years, and I had resolved *not* to get married again. I realized that if I *were* to get married again, I would be on my third husband by the time I was twenty-five! Scary thought. But now, I couldn't find a babysitter *or* a date.

It was the middle of May in 1975 when Jane, my marijuana-smoking friend, and I pulled up to a local bar and stepped out into seventy-eight-degree temperatures under a partly cloudy sky. Since it was only 5:00 p.m., there were plenty of tables available, and the only sounds were soft-spoken conversations and glasses clanging behind the bar. After she ordered a scotch and water on the rocks, I ordered the same thing. Jane raised her eyebrows. "What happened to the Tom Collins?"

"I'm trying to get used to scotch and water," I said. Jane shrugged her shoulders and didn't say anymore. Everyone drank scotch and water, and no one drank Tom Collins. The waitress set two napkins on the table and then placed two scotch and waters (on the rocks) on top of them. When I took a sip, my face scrunched, my head shook, and I breathed through my mouth. I lit a cigarette and set it in the ashtray before settling back in my chair with my arms crossed.

I watched Jane fluff out her hair and look around the room. "Do you ever think about getting married?" I asked.

"Nope," she said as she lit her cigarette and blew smoke into the air. "Do you?"

"I haven't—I mean—I haven't wanted to, but I feel—well—I feel kinda stuck."

"Uh—not a good reason." Jane lifted her drink to her mouth.

"Survival isn't a good reason?" I asked with a sneer on my face and a tilted head.

Jane rolled her eyes and waved her hand. "You seem to be doing pretty good to me." Her eyes flitted around the room.

I didn't tell Jane about what happened with the Italian guy or what the doctor said or that Fern wanted to quit.

"I'm not talking about marrying *anybody*. I'm just saying that *if* I happen to meet someone I'm attracted to, I think I'll quit my Rafter's job." I picked up my lipstick-covered cigarette and took a drag. "You know—it's hard to get to know someone when you're working all the time."

Jane smashed out her cigarette and scooted her chair back. "I'll be back in a sec." She stood up and trotted off toward the restroom.

I leaned over my scotch and water and rested my forearms on the table as I used the little wooden stirrer to swirl ice around the light brown liquid. I put my right elbow on the table, plopped my chin down on the palm of my hand, and pressed my fingers against my cheek as I stared at the table. *If I were to get married again, I would want the guy to have three things: first, he must be a hard worker; second, he must not lie; and third, he must believe in God.* I took another sip of the scotch and water. It didn't make me shake this time, and I felt a little lightheaded. I slouched back in my chair, crossed my arms, laid my head on the back of the chair, and closed my eyes. *God, please—PLEASE bring me either a husband or a babysitter.*

◆ ◆ ◆

The next week, I noticed two guys at the vending machine during the 10:00 a.m. break and the 2:00 p.m. break at Cessna. I sized up each of them and decided that the one with thick, dark hair and glasses was cuter. Within a few days, I stood in line at the Xerox machine, and the cute guy with glasses stood behind me. A skinny, middle-aged gal with curly, light-brown hair pranced by and swatted the cute guy on the rump. She turned back to him and giggled. I turned my attention to the Xerox machine and wondered what was taking so long, so I stepped to the side and looked down the line at a balding man who stood in front of the machine loading one page after another.

I turned to the cute guy behind me. "I hope that machine has a hell of a lot of ink!" The cute guy chuckled, so I grabbed the opportunity. I found out he liked to go to the Brookside Club, and he'd never been to the Rafters. I told him I worked there on the weekends, and with a light touch on his arm and a smile, I said, "You should come up."

✦ ✦ ✦

The Rafter's was on the top floor, so for the entire weekend, I kept my eyes on each group of people who stepped off the elevator and into the club. The cute guy never showed up. When I spotted him the next week at Cessna, I just turned away when I noticed him coming down the hall.

By ten o'clock the following Friday night, the club was in full swing. Soft conversations had turned to boisterous laughter. The smell of cigarette smoke and alcohol wafted throughout the club, and the bartender flew from one customer to another depositing drinks and swishing glasses in soapy water. I delivered a trayful of drinks and trotted to the cigarette machine beside the elevator to get a pack of cigarettes for a customer. After I deposited two quarters, I pulled the knob for a pack of Winston cigarettes. On my way back to the table, I tucked the empty tray under my arm, so I could open the cigarette package. I unwound the cellophane, tore the silver foil off one end of the package, and tapped the end so that three or four cigarettes stuck out. I arranged them so that one jutted out more than the others, and with a smile, I handed the pack to the customer. When I headed back to the bar, I did a double take when I spotted the cute guy from Cessna sitting at one of my tables with his tall, skinny friend in horn-rimmed glasses. For the next four hours, I brought him one scotch and water after another, but he kept quiet and reserved. Toward the end of the evening, I handed him the tab, and he muttered, "Would you—"

"I'm sorry, I can't hear you." I leaned closer to him with my ear toward his mouth.

"I mean, would you—would you…" His face flushed, and he kept his eyes glued to the table.

I finally understood. With a loud voice, I responded. "If you're asking me out to breakfast, the answer is 'yes.'" He raised his eyes, and for the first time, I noticed he had a radiant smile. "Wait for me in the lobby because they shut the elevators off to this floor at 3:00."

✦ ✦ ✦

The cute guy with glasses opened the passenger door of his red Pacer, and I climbed in. We drove to the Pancake House on Kellogg and settled into a red vinyl booth. Florescent lighting, the smell of sausage and eggs, and the murmur of the couple in the next booth created just the right ambiance to unwind and get to know each other. The gum-chewing waitress in a red and white-striped apron took the pencil from behind her ear and took our order.

What was different about this guy was what he *didn't* do. Allan didn't joke, he didn't play around, and he didn't flirt. When I looked across the booth and into his brown eyes that were outlined with wire-rimmed glasses, I knew he was serious-minded, and I'd better not be flippant with him. I detailed Jenny's disabilities and medical issues, and he nodded and made strong eye contact. When he opened up about himself, his eyes glowed as he told me he tried to get to work before anyone else, and he stayed at work longer than anyone else because he wanted to get ahead. I started to get my hopes up.

When I asked him if he was dating anyone, he said, "Not really."

"Not really?" I shifted my body, leaned toward him with my chin propped up with my palm, and stared at him.

"Well, this girl comes over every once in a while." A flush crept across his face. "I'm not dating her, and I don't really like her."

"How do you know her?" I asked.

"Well, she's my friend's wife, and she came to my apartment once because she was upset about something." He fidgeted and squirmed, but all I saw was that he was honest.

I sure didn't want him asking *me* these types of questions, so I changed the subject. Allan's face showed gratitude, and his body relaxed.

"I pray for Jenny, and God sure takes care of her," I said. I took another drink of my Coke and a drag off my cigarette.

Allan leaned back, relaxed, and blew smoke into the air. "I'm an agnostic."

"You're a what?"

He smashed out his cigarette and leaned into the table with both forearms crossed over. "I'm agnostic. That means I don't know if there *is* a God, and I don't really care one way or another." Allan cocked his head to the side with a smirk on his face.

I just crossed my arms and stared back at him. *Well, he's a hard worker, and he's honest. Two out of three isn't bad.*

# CHAPTER TWENTY-THREE

The next Tuesday, Allan parked his red Pacer in front of the sidewalk that led to my apartment door. He carried a bag of Mexican food in one hand and knocked on my door with the other. Inside my apartment, beams of sunlight waltzed through the back window and cast a pleasant glare over the small dinette. It was a perfect seventy-five-degree evening, so I opened the back door. When Allan stepped inside, the tasty smells of taco sauce and chili powder blended with the warm breeze. Allan held Jenny while I pulled plates from the cabinet and filled glasses with ice and Coke. I took Jenny out of Allan's arms, situated her on my lap, and wrapped a bib around her neck. I smashed out my cigarette, swiped her spoon across mushed green beans, and dipped the end into the fruit. Then, I worked the food into her mouth. After that, I laid the spoon down and took a bite out of my taco. I alternated back and forth, but Jenny didn't take her last bite until thirty minutes after Allan and I had finished eating, and the dishes were washed and put away.

Allan told me he was divorced, but his bitter ex-wife wouldn't let him see his three-year-old daughter. He had joined the Air Force right out of high school and had gone to Vietnam. After that, he was stationed in Ipswich, England. I told him all about Tony, but I *didn't* tell him about my current reputation. Then—my phone rang.

I held Jenny as I navigated around the table, through the hall, and into the back bedroom. I picked up the avocado receiver, and I could feel my face burn when I heard the voice of the high-powered lawyer. He had called me earlier, and now he was calling again. I scraped my fingers through my hair and glanced back and forth from the doorway to the phone.

"You can't call me," I said. I turned away from the door, covered the mouthpiece with my left hand, and spoke in a low voice. "You better not mess this up for me!" He finally got the message and hung up.

When I moseyed back into the living room, I noticed that Allan had moved from the kitchen chair and onto the navy-blue, floral sofa. I smiled, but he avoided eye contact and cleared his throat. After a moment, he leaned forward with his forearms resting on his knees and his fingers laced together. When he looked at me, his eyes narrowed in confusion. I knew I had to tell him.

"Um—I need to tell you something." I meandered around the coffee table and sat on the opposite end of the couch with Jenny on my lap. "I told you that Tony used to mess around on me."

Allan stiffened and furrowed his brow. "Yeah."

"Well—I always felt that it was better to *know* what was going on rather than be the ignorant wife left at home." Allan rubbed his forehead and gave me a dazed look. "So," I continued, "I thought it was much better for me to use men for sex rather than letting *them* have all the control."

Allan's head shot up, and he tilted his head in confusion. "You thought it was better for *you* to *use* men for sex?"

"Yeah," I said. I winced as I avoided eye contact with him and stared down at Jenny. "The mistress knows the guy much better than the wife does—you know."

Allan's eyes were glued to my face, and he lifted one eyebrow. "You really thought you could *use* men for sex?" He seemed at a loss for words.

I turned to him, and my eyes widened. "Well—yeah." My head flinched back slightly. "I just thought you should know because—I—I've been with quite a few guys."

All of a sudden, Allan started to snicker. My eyebrows came together in confusion. "Are you laughing?"

"I'm sorry," he said. He cleared his throat and tried to make his face look serious, but he couldn't retain it. His chuckle turned into uncontrollable laughter.

"So, you don't think I'm terrible?" I asked.

Allan wiped tears from his eyes and was finally able to talk. "No, I don't think you're terrible," he said. "I think you're very stu—uh—naïve."

My whole body collapsed with relief. The next weekend, I gave the Rafters my two-week notice.

◆ ◆ ◆

A week later, we decided Allan should move in. He seemed oblivious to the dust, dirt, and moldy shower in his apartment, and I didn't like going there. His lease was up, and since he spent every night with me anyway, it was senseless for him to keep it.

The next Saturday, I scrubbed the bathroom and kitchen with Bab-O, wiped down furniture with Johnson Pledge Furniture Polish, and vacuumed the carpet. It was eighty degrees and sunny, so I opened the back door. The apartment sparkled and smelled like furniture polish, and a warm breeze glided through the air. Then, I loaded my Torino with a basketful of clothes, set Jenny in the back seat, and drove to the laundry mat. While I was gone, Allan stacked his things into his red Pacer, drove to my apartment, and took his things out of his car and into my apartment.

I hummed and smiled as I took Jenny out of her travel chair and carried her to the door. When I opened the door, the humming and singing stopped, and my mouth fell open.

A mountain of stuff that I didn't recognize filled half the living room. "What the hell is all this?" I shot out my arm and swept my hand toward the mountain. Allan stood beside a pile of clothes, tennis rackets, tennis balls, pots, pans, dishes, and bedding.

He jerked his head back and gave me a dazed look. "What do you mean?—It's my stuff!" He grabbed his pack of Marlboros off the coffee table, took out a cigarette, and lit it. He blew smoke up into the air, turned to me, and scrutinized my face. I breathed hard and shook my head as I laid Jenny on the sofa and stomped back out the door to get the laundry basket full of folded clothes. With narrowed eyes that darted toward the pile and then to Allan, I barged through the living room and into the bedroom. I put clothes away and emptied a drawer for Allan before I reentered the living room in a huff.

"I don't have room for all this crap!"

Allan stepped back, and his body became rigid. "What the hell did you expect me to do?" he said. "I have no idea where you wanted me to put this stuff!" He smashed out his cigarette in the ashtray, stood up, and folded his arms. His eyes bore into mine. For some reason, I had not thought about all the things he'd be bringing with him when he moved out of his apartment. We stared at each other, and he finally broke the silence.

"Does this apartment complex have some sort of storage?" he asked.

"I have no idea." My shoulders began to relax at the thought that there might be a storage area, and I lit a cigarette. "I'll have to call Mrs. Feather."

"Who's Mrs. Feather?"

"The apartment manager," I said. "She'll be furious when she finds out I'm living with someone, though."

The following Monday, I called Mrs. Feather and found out there was a storage area for my apartment in the basement. I didn't even know there *was* a basement. We found the doorway and stepped down creaky stairs and into a dark, musty basement with spider webs hanging from the ceiling and around windows. I unlocked the padlock on a unit made of boards and chicken wire. This was perfect!

# CHAPTER TWENTY-FOUR

During one of Jenny's hospital stays, a confident white-uniformed nurse pranced into Jenny's room and held out her arms for me to hand Jenny over. She checked her breathing and took her temperature before she handed her back to me. Out in the hall, food carts rattled and clanged as they rolled up and down the hallway, and the smell of dinner floated into each hospital room. I sat on brown and gold-plaid cushions that covered a wooden rocker. The cushions were attached to the rocker with plaid bows that were tied around each back post. I sat Jenny on my lap and adjusted her bib before I picked up her spoon half filled with meat and vegetables. I squeezed the food into Jenny's mouth and rubbed my fingers under her chin to get her to swallow. The nurse stopped scribbling on her chart and studied how I fed Jenny.

"Have you ever thought about a gastrostomy tube?" she asked.

"What's a gastrostomy tube?" I kept my eyes on Jenny and continued to rub and prod.

"It's a feeding tube that's inserted directly into her stomach," she said. I stopped what I was doing, raised my eyebrows, and analyzed her face. When she glanced up from her chart, she saw that my eyes watched her with sudden focus.

"You could feed her liquid food through the gastrostomy tube." The self-assured nurse turned her attention back to her chart and glided her pen across blank boxes and over black lines. After an exaggerated sweep, she clicked the end of her pen with her thumb, attached it to her chart, and turned her attention back to me. "You should ask Dr. Robinson about it." A moment later, she swung her head around and trotted out the door. My eyes followed her until the door closed. *I wonder why no one ever told me this before.*

When I asked Dr. Robinson about it, he seemed hesitant, and I didn't think to ask why. All I knew was that I could get the much-needed nutrition down her, and she would probably stop getting pneumonia so much. After much imploring, Dr. Robinson gave me the name of a surgeon, and I scheduled Jenny's surgery to take place right after her third birthday.

◆ ◆ ◆

It was a cloudy day in late June, and the temperature was already in the seventies when I wheeled Jenny into the hospital. The hospital had the usual fluorescent lighting, smells of antiseptic and floor wax, and white-uniformed nurses with white caps who marched up and down the shiny-tiled hallways. Allan and I stopped in front of the gray-haired receptionist, and I gave her Jenny's name and showed her my insurance card. She waved her hand toward the elevators and told us how to find the surgical floor. Within thirty minutes, a surgical assistant dressed in a green gown with a white cap wrapped around his forehead appeared at the waiting room door. Holding a brown clipboard, he scanned the room and called out Jenny's name. He stood by patiently while I gave Jenny a hug and kiss before I laid her in the arms of the assistant. When Allan asked where we were supposed to wait, he shifted Jenny into the crook of his left arm, and with his right hand, he pointed toward the door and told us to go down this hall and then turn right and go down that hall.

End tables topped with a smattering of magazines such as *Life* and *Popular Science* sat at the end of a row of brown vinyl chairs with metal armrests. I sat in one of the chairs, crossed my legs, and swung my foot back and forth while I mindlessly glanced at and flipped through a *Seventeen* magazine. I finally gave up, threw it back on the end table, and asked Allan what time it was.

An hour after I had handed Jenny over to the assistant, a fifty-something, green-gowned surgeon with thinning black hair stood at the door of the waiting room and called for the mother of Jennifer. I raised my hand and headed toward him. He told me the surgery was finished, everything went well, and I could see her in about ten minutes.

Fifteen minutes later, I stepped carefully into the recovery room. Everything was immaculate, white, and smelled of disinfectant. The white-uniformed nurse smiled at me and pointed to where Jenny lay. I tiptoed to the pediatric hospital crib. Jenny's entire body was swathed in several white blankets, and she lay on her side with her eyes closed. I laid my hand gently on her bottom and leaned my face close to hers. "Hi, there," I whispered. I could see rolling movement underneath swollen eyelids. I rubbed her bottom ever so gently as I stared at her face. Her light-brown hair was swept off to the side, and her face was ashen and puffy.

I lifted my head and turned to the nurse. "How long will it be before the anesthesia wears off?" I asked. Before she could answer, my face was back down in front of Jenny's.

The nurse reached for Jenny's paperwork and flipped through it. "It doesn't look like they gave her any anesthesia."

My head shot up, and my body froze. "What did you say?"

The nurse was focused on the logistics of her paperwork and didn't notice that my mouth fell open and my eyes bulged. "Let's see. It looks like Jenny is already taking phenobarbital and Dilantin, and they don't like giving too much anesthetics to babies and children."

"Jenny's been on phenobarbital and Dilantin for a long time," I said. My heart caved into my chest when I thought of what they had done to her with no pain medicine. My eyes filled with tears, and I laid my face back close to hers.

◆ ◆ ◆

Two days later, Jenny was in her hospital room, and a dark-haired pediatric nurse shuffled into the room carrying a syringe wrapped in cellophane, a cylinder-shaped food container, Q-tips, Zephiran,

Betadine, cotton balls, and alcohol. After she laid everything down on the table next to Jenny's bed, she stuck out her hand and introduced herself. "I'm here to show you how to feed Jenny and take care of her tube." She handed me a sheet of detailed instructions.

Jenny was responsive now, so I was ready. I picked up the white sheet filled with written instructions alongside cartoon-type drawings. I fixated on trying to coordinate the written instructions with everything she said and did.

She swung her head toward Jenny and looked up and down Jenny's body. "Before you feed her, you have to elevate her head," she said. She made sure Jenny was face-up and grabbed a large, fluffy pillow and put it under Jenny's head at a forty-five-degree angle so that the rest of her body slanted down. She said I needed to allow forty-five minutes to feed her and another forty-five minutes of rest with her head slanted up. Afterward, I had to reverse her and put her on her side or stomach. To show me, she pulled the pillow out from under Jenny's head and put it under her hips and legs so that her head slanted down. "Like this," she said. "This position helps prevent phlegm from settling into her lungs." Since she was about to show me how to feed her, she took the pillow out from under her legs and put it back under her head.

The nurse lifted Jenny's tube off the bed, took a syringe, and stuck it into the end of the tube. Then, she pulled up on the end of the syringe. "Before feeding her, you have to use the syringe to withdraw air from the tube until you see some gastric juices," she said. She then disconnected the syringe and held it in front of my face. She put the syringe back on the end table, reached for the food container, and

FOR THE LOVE OF GOD

attached Jenny's gastrostomy tube to the tip on the end of the food container. "Be sure to put her medicines into the food container first, so the liquid food will push the medicine through." The nurse then told me that beginning at 6:00 in the morning and until 10:00 at night, Jenny needed to be fed every three or four hours. When she saw me flinch and my body stiffen, she reiterated: "Yes—every three or four hours."

The pediatric nurse then strode over to the sink and ran cool water over a small washcloth. She used the wet washcloth to both moisten Jenny's mouth and wipe it out. If she was thirsty, Jenny could suck on it. Then, she cleaned the tube itself with cotton balls and alcohol.

The nurse undressed Jenny and examined the area around her gastrostomy tube.

"You have to soak the skin around the tube with Zephiran until all the gunk is loosened," she said. She soaked several Q-tips in Zephiran and gently pressed the soaked cotton tips on Jenny's skin around her new tube. Then, she patted it dry. After that, she soaked several other Q-tips in Betadine and wiped them over all the cleansed skin areas around the tube. Lastly, she taped the tube so it wouldn't come out. "You'll have to do this in the morning and at night," she said. "Any questions?"

"Nope." I stuck out my hand and gave her a firm handshake.

She left the Q-tips, Zephiran, Betadine, cotton balls, and alcohol and headed to the door. While her hand was still on the doorknob, she lifted her head and turned back to me as if she needed to tell me something.

"You might want to keep an eye on the area around the tube

because it looks a little red," she said. "If Jenny starts to run a fever, be sure to tell the doctor."

The next day, Jenny had a fever of 102.

# CHAPTER TWENTY-FIVE

The surgeon with black, thinning hair leaned over Jenny, pulled up her thin pink cotton gown, and dabbed his fingers cautiously around the skin that encircled the gastrostomy tube. After he fidgeted with the tube, he lifted his head and gave a crisp nod. "Everything looks good!"

I cleared my throat. "But she started running a fever this morning."

He stopped scrawling on his brown clipboard and studied my face. "You'll need to talk to your pediatrician about that." His eyes returned to his clipboard. "The fever has nothing to do with the surgery." He wheeled around and set off toward the door with a steady gait.

After he closed the door, I asked a white-capped nurse to call Dr. Robinson. A couple of hours later, she strutted back into Jenny's room. "Dr. Robinson said you need to talk to the surgeon about it."

"Well, that's just great." My face began to burn, and I rubbed my eyebrows. "Is there another doctor on duty right now that I could talk to?" The nurse set up a consultation with a doctor I'd never met.

Allan and I stepped into a doctor's office that smelled of cigarette smoke and coffee. The small space contained a metal desk piled with medical journals, folders, and a white ceramic ashtray. Behind the desk was a black vinyl swivel chair, and in front of the desk were two empty chairs. We settled in and waited for the doctor. A few moments later, the doctor popped into the room and shut the door behind him. The heavyset doctor was fifty-some-odd years old and dressed in the typical white lab coat. After quick introductions, he stepped behind his desk and lit a cigarette. He took a deep drag and blew smoke into the air before placing it in the white ceramic ashtray. He leaned back in his vinyl swivel chair, placed his hands on his paunch, and laced his fingers. "I've read Jennifer's chart, and it looks like she came through the surgery pretty well." I nodded and waited. He rocked back and forth in his swivel chair, and then he leaned forward and clicked his fingernails on his desk. "I'm not sure what else you want me to do."

"She has a fever." I felt my head begin to ache. "When I talked to the surgeon about it, he said I needed to talk to my pediatrician, but my pediatrician said it's because of the surgery." When the heavyset doctor didn't respond, I looked down at my hands, but Allan glared at the doctor.

The doctor took another drag of his cigarette. "As you know, Jennifer has a lot of medical problems." He paused and waited for me to respond. I started to say something but decided to keep my mouth shut. He continued. "—and it doesn't look as if either of her doctors seem to think further treatment is necessary—*so*, I don't know what you expect from me." He took another drag from his cigarette and glanced up at the wall clock. His forehead furrowed.

Allan leaned in toward the doctor with both forearms on his legs and his fingers crisscrossed. A flush crept up his face, and his jaw tightened. "What we want—," he said with an added pause, "is for you to *stop* treating her like a sack of potatoes and *start* treating her like a human being."

I raised my eyebrows and swung my head toward Allan. The doctor's eyes also turned to Allan and stared daggers. Allan continued to lean forward with his forearms on his knees and his fingers still intertwined. He didn't move, and he didn't blink. After a few moments, the doctor's knee started to bounce. "I'll have the nurses order some antibiotics for her." He got up, snatched his chart off his desk, and marched out the door.

◆ ◆ ◆

Allan and I had been living together for about three weeks when my mom called and said she was coming for a visit at the end of July. That meant she would be staying with me for a whole week. When I asked Allan what he thought we should do, his head flinched back slightly. "Hell if I know."

A few days later, it was the first week of July, and I stood in the kitchen and gathered baby jars of green beans and meat and pulled milk out of the refrigerator. It was about 5:00 in the evening and a warm eighty-six degrees, so the window air conditioner hummed. My spoon clanged against the glass bowl as I mixed Jenny's food with milk to pour into her gastrostomy container.

Allan sat on one of the dinette chairs and studied me. All of a sudden, he stood up. "I need to talk to you." I strode past him to get Jenny, but he grabbed my arm. "I need you to pay attention." His face was grave, and I knew I needed to stop what I was doing and listen to him.

Ever since Allan strolled through my front door with that sack of Mexican food, I had assumed that we would get married.

I faced him and gave him my full attention. "What?"

Allan put both his hands on my shoulders. "I—I want you to marry me." He peered into my eyes with all seriousness.

"Of course, we'll get married," I said. His eyebrows rose and his mouth clamped shut. I proceeded to the couch and picked up Jenny to get her ready to feed. "We *could* get married before Mom comes," I said. "That way, you won't have to go anywhere when she gets here."

He seemed to resign himself to my nonchalant response to his proposal, and we pulled down the calendar that hung on the side of the upper, white cabinet.

Allan stood solidly and stared down at me with strong eye contact. "We can't tell *anyone*." I knew the reason. Both our parents, along with Aunt Lee and Uncle Gilbert, would be appalled to find out we got married after knowing each other for only six weeks.

❖ ❖ ❖

July 11 was on a Friday. After I fed Jenny that evening, I dressed her in a frilly pink dress and dressed myself in a polyester turquoise and white plaid pantsuit. Allan changed into a collared yellow, short-sleeved knit shirt and brown-plaid, polyester bell bottoms. At five o'clock, we stepped out of the apartment, and I rolled Jenny to the car in her travel chair. After I got her situated, I straightened her dress so it wouldn't wrinkle. Allan climbed into the driver's seat of my brown Torino, and I spread the paper map out on my lap and found the address for the justice of the peace in Maize, Kansas. We passed by stores, then houses, and then nothing except flat farmland. Eventually, we pulled up to an old, dinky, white-framed house with a roomy front porch.

The short, stout, gray-haired man beamed as he opened the screen door to let us in. A bedroom was right off the living room, and when I laid Jenny on the bed, Mr. Stone lit up when he saw the gastrostomy tube. I did a double-take when I saw his reaction.

"Is this a gastrostomy tube?" he asked. His eyes softened, and he spoke gently to Jenny as he reached for her hand and wiggled it. "What's wrong with her?"

I marveled at his reaction. He wasn't afraid of her at all. "She's profoundly brain damaged." He continued to smile and speak gently to her.

"My wife had a gastrostomy tube put in before she died." His voice started to break, and his shoulders drooped. "She's been gone now for almost a year." He released Jenny's hand and turned his attention to Allan and me.

"You'll need a couple of witnesses." Our eyes widened, and we just stood there with nervous grins. He just waved his hand and wheeled around toward the front door. "We can try to flag someone down off the street." We stepped onto the porch and lit up a couple of cigarettes before we sat on a couple of white wooden rocking chairs. Even though it was eighty degrees, the breeze and clear skies made the evening perfect. The air smelled of moist soil and mowed hay. Mr. Stone placed an ashtray and a couple of glasses of iced tea on a small white table before he slouched back into a third rocking chair. His eyes brightened when he spoke of his wife and told stories about their life together. He seemed to enjoy the company and lost interest in finding us a couple of witnesses. Thirty minutes later, we still hadn't seen a single car drive down the narrow, paved street in front of his house.

"Is there something else we can try?" Allan asked.

"Well, we can drive down to a restaurant, but that's about—well— let's see." He looked off into nothing. "I'd say it's about a mile from here. There might be a couple of people there."

"Would we get married in the restaurant?" Allan's eyes widened, and his eyebrows shot up as he glanced toward me.

"Well—you *could*," Mr. Stone said. "Unless, of course, they would be willing to come back here."

Allan started to fidget. "Let's just see if someone comes." I stroked Jenny's hair and bit my lower lip.

About ten minutes later, Allan saw a car coming, so he rushed to the street and waved his arms every which way. A couple of scruffy-looking boys in their late teens stepped out of the car and eagerly agreed to stand beside us and sign a piece of paper for ten dollars each.

❖ ❖ ❖

Heavy curtains blocked out the remaining evening sunlight, so Mr. Stone pulled the chain on a stained-glass lamp, and the living room became quiet and solemn. The reminiscent smell of the past saturated the room. Mr. Stone's demeanor changed from good-natured to somber. He pointed to a couple of chairs off in the corner for the boys, and I grasped a pillow from the corner of the sofa and situated it under Jenny's head. Mr. Stone guided us to the center of the room and put his hands on our shoulders to turn each of us toward him. Allan stood to my left, and Mr. Stone stood in front of us and wrapped the ends of his wire-framed glasses around his ears. When Mr. Stone opened the Bible, the feeling of solidarity and reverence seemed almost tangible. It was just the three of us standing there, and everything else faded into the background. He spoke about the importance of the vow we were making before God. He stressed that God had designed marriage as a permanent union between a man and a woman, and we should no longer think of ourselves as two separate people but as one integrated unit. I stood quietly and gave a slow nod every time he mentioned God and the seriousness of this occasion. I didn't understand most of what he said, but I *did* understand that I was making a vow before God, so I'd better not take this lightly. After we exchanged vows and rings, he closed the Bible and shook our hands. We handed the boys their money, and we handed Mr. Stone thirty dollars.

❖ ❖ ❖

We drove back down the narrow road to the Diamond Inn restaurant. The restaurant was dark, and the sound of music from the 1940s united with the smell of charcoaled steak and baked potatoes. This combination made the restaurant a popular go-to place for gray-haired couples. I laid Jenny beside me in the vinyl, dark-red booth and ordered steak and lobster. After dinner, the waitress laid the check in front of Allan and trotted off. He picked it up and gave a heavy sigh. When he calculated a 10 percent tip to the penny, my head jerked. "What are you doing?"

He glanced at me as he leaned sideways to dig out change from his pants pocket. "I'm leaving a tip." I gave him an incredulous stare.

I shook my head and reached for my purse. "I'm glad my customers at the Rafters didn't do that."

# CHAPTER TWENTY-SIX

When I was single, once a week, I would drive to the gas station, and after the tank was full, I'd hand the attendant cash from my weekend tip money. I also used tip money for groceries and anything else that wasn't some sort of bill. Every two weeks, Myrna handed me my paycheck from Cessna, and I would drive up to the bank's bulletproof window. I signed the back of the check and laid it in the metal tray for the teller. All tip money went to groceries, gas, and any other type of odds and ends, and Cessna money went to bills. I paid bills according to the order of importance: rent, utilities, Dr. Robinson, and other medical bills. It was simple. If the total bill was X amount of money, I would write a check for X amount of money. It never entered my mind that there would be any other way to pay a bill. Also, I never once took Jenny to Dr. Robinson's office or the hospital and thought, *"This is going to cost money."*

On the other hand, Allan and money had a different relationship—and a bit contradictory. My first introduction to Allan and money now seems contradictory. It was the second night we were together, and he had brought over Mexican food. After we ate, cleaned the kitchen, and I had tucked Jenny in bed, I sat beside Allan on the navy-flowered sofa in the living room. The room smelled of Mexican food and baby powder. It was beginning to get dark, so I turned the switch on the white ceramic lamp that was next to the ashtray on the end table. Allan lit a couple of cigarettes and handed me one. In the course of the conversation, we started to chat about money.

"I stick my head out the car window to dry my hair," he said.

My head flinched back slightly. "Why? Hairdryers aren't that expensive." Allan just shrugged his shoulders and took another drag off his cigarette.

For some reason, I decided to show him all my medical bills. I flipped the switch for the dining room light and pulled white envelopes out of the kitchen drawer. I knelt in front of the coffee table and lined up white sheets of medical invoices in rows across the green shag carpet. Allan reached down and picked up each sheet. I watched his eyes scan through each bill and stop when he reached the bold number at the bottom of the invoice. He shook his head a little before laying it back down and leaning toward the next bill. After he laid the last one down, I gathered them up and tapped the sheets of white paper on the top of the dinette table. I shrugged my shoulders. "It's no big deal." I felt Allan's eyes follow me, so I turned and saw him watch me and pinch his chin.

I tilted my head back and looked directly at him. "Really—it's no big deal."

"You've got about five hundred dollars' worth of bills there."

"I know, but trust me—I'm not worried about it *at all!*" I strutted toward the TV and turned the knob to the right. Allan followed right behind me, leaned over my shoulder, and turned the knob to the left. I spun around.

"I've got five hundred dollars in the bank."

I jerked my head back, and my eyes widened. "No—I'm not asking for money."

"I know you're not."

A few days later, I handed the bank teller five hundred dollars through the bulletproof window, and that night, I wrote checks for every one of the medical bills that I had laid across the carpet.

◆ ◆ ◆

Jenny's chest deflated with each breath, so I figured she had pneumonia.

Dr. Robinson wrapped his stethoscope around his neck. "She has pneumonia in both lungs, so she'll have to be admitted." I let out a sigh of relief. *No babysitter worries this week.*

The dark-haired lady with glasses propped on the end of her nose admitted her and handed me the admission papers. She leaned toward the glass and pointed a bony finger with red nail polish toward the door. "Go through this door, and they'll prep her and take her to the ICU."

Jenny's head lay on my shoulder, and I could feel myself smiling. She received much better care in the Intensive Care Unit than she did on the floor.

After Jenny was settled in, I made sure the head nurse knew how to take care of her.

"Jenny's head has to be raised for forty-five minutes after she eats and lowered for forty-five minutes after that." The nurse watched my every move and nodded as another nurse set up the suction machine beside her bed.

I eyed the nurse with the suction machine. "She uses a size seven French suction tube," I said.

◆ ◆ ◆

The next morning, Allan and I strolled down the hall toward Jenny's room. Food carts rattled and tiled floors gleamed. Nurses in starched white uniforms and white caps toted plates of eggs, bacon, and toast into patients' rooms. Without warning, a nurse popped up out of nowhere, scurried toward us, and stopped us before we reached Jenny's room. Her arms and shoulders were tense, and she glanced around uneasily. She pointed to an empty room off to the side, and we followed her in. She closed the door.

"Last night, a code blue was called on Jenny." She cleared her throat, and her eyes flitted from me to Allan and back to me.

My eyes narrowed. "What's a code blue?"

"Well—it's a—it's when a patient needs to be resuscitated."

My head flinched back, and my eyebrows squished together. "I don't know what you mean."

"I mean—Jenny stopped breathing, and we had to call in the medical team to bring her back."

I took a couple of steps back, and my voice shook. "Back—back to life?" My heart stopped beating. "Is—is she OK?" I felt my throat constrict as hot tears welled up.

The nurse hesitated and ran her hands down the front of her white uniform to smooth out wrinkles that weren't there. "She's stable now, but we'll have to watch her closely." She rubbed my back before she wandered toward the door. Her hand wrapped around the metal door handle, and she glanced back at me with a sympathetic smile. "I'm so sorry."

I bit my lip, and my posture stooped. I turned to Allan with desperation in my eyes. "Will you pray for her?" Allan's gaze clouded over, and his thoughts seemed distant. "Please pray for her!" I repeated. Allan's eyes jerked back to me, and he nodded.

Jenny's fever broke later that day, and by the next day, she was almost back to normal. She was soon out of the ICU and back in a regular room.

I rocked Jenny and ran my fingers through her light-brown hair. "Did you pray for her?"

Allan glanced around the room uneasily. "Yes."

I reached over Jenny, took the last drag off my cigarette, and crushed it out. I smiled down at Jenny. I knew that Allan was no longer an agnostic.

✦ ✦ ✦

After work, Allan held the door open as I gathered the white envelopes that stuck out of the mailbox. I threw the white envelopes on the kitchen table and laid Jenny on the sofa. It was ninety degrees outside, so the air conditioner hummed and sunlight streamed in from the back window. After I got Jenny arranged and her liquid food started, I ripped open the white envelopes and pulled out medical bills. I went completely still, and my eyes fixated on the bolded words *Past Due*, which were alongside Dr. Robinson's name.

"What the *hell* is this?"

Allan jerked his head in my direction. "What the hell is *what*?"

I stomped toward him and pointed to the words at the bottom of the page. "What the hell is *this*?"

Allan snatched the bill from my hands, and his eyes glanced at the bolded words. His jaw and neck tightened. "I'll get him paid—don't worry about it."

"I damn well *am* going to worry about it!" I marched up to him and bared my teeth. "Dr. Robinson *always* gets paid—and he gets paid first!" My eyes were cold and hard.

Allan held his chin high, and his face reddened. "Dr. Robinson and these medical people *do* take partial payments, you know."

"I don't *care*!" My heart raced to the point where it almost felt painful. I could feel my eyes begin to burn and water.

When Allan saw me, the redness in his face faded and his chin lowered. "I'll get a check in the mail tomorrow," he said. "But you don't *have* to pay the full amount on medical bills."

I pushed back my shoulders and stood firm. "I will *always* pay Dr. Robinson as soon as I get the bill, and I will *always* pay him the full amount." I turned, picked up Jenny, and carried her to the bedroom.

# CHAPTER TWENTY-SEVEN

On a Friday night at the end of July, we scanned the newspaper for movies at the drive-in theaters. My index finger landed on the Meadow Lark Drive-In, so I fed and bathed Jenny, dressed her in pink, lightweight cotton pajamas, and we headed to the movie. We handed the freckle-faced teenager four dollars, and the tires crunched over gravel as we drove in and out through rows of parked cars until we found a spot. Allan pulled up beside a speaker, rolled down his window, and hooked the back of the metal speaker over the edge of his window so it was facing inside the car. He adjusted his window to fit the speaker just so, and he turned the knob on the bottom of the speaker to make sure it worked. We rolled down the rest of the windows and let the warm eighty-five-degree breeze waft through my Torino. We leaned our seats back and turned our eyes to the gigantic, white screen with rows of swings right beneath it. We watched kids run and climb on and off swings. The older kids knew to stretch out their legs as high as they could on their way forward to grab air and tuck them under on the way back to make the swing go higher and higher. The screams got louder as the kids soared higher. At about 8:30, the screen lit up, and kids jumped off the swings and ran back to smoke-filled cars.

Two hours later, it was intermission, and cartoon-type commercials displayed ice-cold drinks, sizzling hamburgers, and popcorn popping. Periodically, a man's voice announced, "The show starts in … minutes." Allan lifted Jenny out of her travel chair, laid her head on his shoulder, and we traipsed over gravel past parked cars on our way to the concession stand. The smell of popcorn, hot dogs, and the sounds of excited conversations percolated through the glass building that was designated as the concession stand. I grabbed a red and white box of popcorn, filled two paper cups with ice and Coke, and set everything on a red plastic tray. We shuffled by a line of people until we took our place at the end of the long line. It didn't take much time for new people to line up behind us. I balanced the tray, and Allan held Jenny with her head resting on his shoulder.

"Sir—uh—sir?" said a voice behind us. Allan turned around, and a thirty-something, brown-headed man stood beside a blond woman, and both had huge round eyes and creased foreheads.

"Yeah?" Allan said. With a confused look and a tilted head, he studied their faces trying to figure out what was wrong. "What?" he repeated.

"Um—I think—uh—I think something is wrong with your little girl." Allan leaned back over his shoulder and peered at Jenny. Her eyes were rolling back.

"Oh." Allan's face relaxed. He shifted her to his other shoulder and smiled at them. "She's okay—she's just having a seizure."

They both froze, and their faces turned white.

When he saw their faces, his head jerked. "She's fine—really." Allan turned back to me, and our mouths curved up into a knowing smile.

◆ ◆ ◆

A patient nurse once showed me how to help Jenny have a bowel movement. She picked up a jar of Vaseline and rubbed some over Jenny's rectum. With her little finger, she gently circled and pushed. "Jenny needs a little encouragement to feel the sensation that she needs to push." She winked at me and cleaned her up. That was over a year ago.

Now, Jenny had been in the hospital for over a week. It was August and ninety-nine degrees outside when I pushed open the glass door to the hospital and stepped into a blast of cool air. Nurses scrambled this way and that chatting with each other and nodding at passing doctors. When I entered Jenny's room, I jerked back the clear plastic tent that served as a barrier to the cool mist that surrounded her bed. After I pulled her out of bed and sat her on my lap, I dipped a cotton swab into cool water and into her mouth. She seemed thirsty, so I dipped more and more water into her mouth. A few minutes later, I checked her diaper.

Instead of having to encourage bowel stimulation, her diaper was filled with orange liquid that had the same consistency and color as the food concoction that flowed through her gastrostomy tube. This had been going on for a while, so when the white-uniformed nurse entered the room, I showed her the orangey liquid in Jenny's diaper.

"What's happening?" I gazed at the nurse and focused on her reaction. "Is she not processing her food or what?"

The nurse glanced down at the contents of the diaper and shrugged her shoulders. "I dunno."

My jaw tightened. "Well, can you *ask* someone?"

Her head flinched back slightly. "Sure—I can ask." She finished taking Jenny's vitals and writing on the form that was clipped to her brown clipboard. She jammed the pencil underneath the clip on the clipboard and avoided my gaze as she set off toward the door. "I'll send in the head nurse."

"Thanks." The head nurse never came in.

◆ ◆ ◆

The next day, Jenny's temperature had not broken, and she still lay inside the mist-filled tent. After work, I stopped by the nurses' station before going into Jenny's room. The nurse behind the desk had a stethoscope wrapped around her neck and a black receiver glued to her ear. She cackled and gabbed as if I was invisible. I propped my elbow on the counter, rested my chin on the fist of my left hand, and finger-tapped the long counter with my right hand. Finally, she giggled goodbye and laid the receiver in the black cradle. With a heavy sigh, she flicked her gaze upward.

"May I help you?"

My eyes went to the name pinned to her white uniform. "Yes—Doris," I said with a forced smile. "Is Dr. Robinson making rounds this evening?"

Doris flipped through some sort of schedule and ran her finger down it. "Yes, he's scheduled to come in this evening." All of a sudden, the tension left my body.

"Thanks!" My smile went from forced to genuine, and I spun around and pranced down the hall toward Jenny's room.

That evening, Dr. Robinson pressed the stethoscope on Jenny's chest and scanned her chart. He remained quiet through the examination and maintained a vacant look. "I'm still hearing some pneumonia." He wrapped the stethoscope back around his neck and wrote on her chart. "She has quite a bit of scarring on her lungs, you know." I nodded.

"Her bowel movements are the same color and texture as the food I mix for her."

He focused on his notes and avoided my dazed look. "Oh yeah?" Dr. Robinson was unusually quiet. The tense feeling that I'd felt all day returned. "There's not much more I can do for her." He drew his mouth into a straight line and bit his lip. "Do you have any suggestions?"

My eyes widened, and I rubbed my arms absentmindedly. *Was Dr. Robinson asking for MY advice?* "Um—uh." My mind started to roll. "Well—uh— we could give her breathing treatments."

"Sure! We can try that." The corners of his mouth turned up, and the room felt lighter. "I'll get the order to the nurses before I leave."

# CHAPTER TWENTY-EIGHT

Except for her diaper, Jenny lay naked across my double bed with her legs partially dropping off the side. Her wet hair smelled of Johnson's baby shampoo and clung to the sides of her face. One of my legs hung off the side of the bed, and the other was curled up under me as I stooped over Jenny and cleaned around her gastrostomy tube. I threw Zephiran-soaked Q-tips and used cotton balls into the small trash container beside the bed. I put my ear to her chest and felt her throat. Yes, she was raspy, so I hooked up her suction machine and gently worked the tube slowly down her throat. Jenny's face grimaced, and her eyebrows furrowed. I slowed down but continued to insert the tube down her nasal passage. I turned the knob on the machine, and the familiar gurgle sound began as I pulled on the tube. Her cries were muffled and broken. My neck and shoulders felt strained, and my throat began to hurt as I continued to slowly pull out the clear tube that was now filling up with red fluid mixed with clear phlegm.

Her face emitted agony. I wiped my forehead with my left forearm. *I have to do this*, I thought. *She could get pneumonia if I don't.* Jenny tried to twist her head away from the gurgling sound, and she tried to cry, but she couldn't. I continued to focus on the reddened phlegm, and my chest caved in. I glanced up. Allan stood at the doorway with an unnatural stillness and a hesitancy to speak. Finally—he did.

"You're hurting her."

My face turned red and jerked up toward the doorway. I could feel pain in my throat and tears well up in my eyes. I shouted at him. "What do you want me to do—do you want me to let her *die?*"

Allan's face contorted, and he turned and strolled back into the living room. I veered my eyes back to Jenny and watched her writhe in pain until the blood and phlegm-filled tube was finally out.

Jenny's face relaxed, and I started thinking. For over three years, I had fought for Jenny's life because I knew she didn't know or care about her disabilities, and she wasn't in pain. As for me, I'd found a love that I never knew existed. She was mine—all mine. But now—she hurt. Now—she suffered. All of a sudden, my posture stiffened, and I stared at the wall. I was no longer fighting for Jenny—I was fighting for myself.

I slithered off the bed and onto my knees. I buried my wet face on top of my crossed arms that rested on the bedspread beside Jenny's legs. *God! I can't—I can't pray that Jenny die. I just want—I just want to give Jenny to You. I will take care of her needs, but I won't do anything extreme anymore. I just want You to take care of her.*

◆ ◆ ◆

I did not drink any liquids after dinner the night before, and I collected my "urine sample in a clean, dry, soap-free jar." It was the last week in August and a warm eighty-five degrees when I toted the jar of urine into the clinic.

I climbed back into the passenger seat of the Torino. "I'm sure it's a fluke." I lit a cigarette and rolled up the car window with the cigarette hanging from my mouth.

"Why do you say that?" Allan glanced over at me and scratched his cheek.

"Well, I tried to get pregnant with my first husband for a year and that didn't take." Allan stiffened and kept his eyes on the road. "And I was with Tony for nearly two years before I got pregnant, and—well—Jenny has problems." I took a drag off my cigarette. In my mind, my explanation continued. *"And who knows how many times I could have gotten pregnant over the last three years?"* Allan's eyebrows squeezed together, and he glanced at me and shook his head. I kept my mouth shut.

Two days later, I laid Jenny on the navy-flowered sofa and pulled the yellow pages out of the white kitchen drawer. I ran my index finger down the page until I stopped on the name of the medical clinic where I had dropped off my urine. I left the phone book open on the counter, and I repeated the number in my head as I sprinted back to the phone in the bedroom. After I planted myself on the edge of the double bed, I picked up the receiver and swirled the rotary dial. After a couple of rings, the receptionist picked up the phone. She took my name and put me on hold. I scraped my fingers through my hair and took quick breaths. A few minutes later, I could hear her phone rumble and clack as she picked it up.

"Mrs. Guinn?"

"Yes?"

"Your test came back positive." When she didn't hear a response, she just said, "Congratulations," and hung up.

I sat there with a flat gaze as I continued to hold the receiver on my lap.

＋ ＋ ＋

When I handed Jenny to new babysitters, I also handed them a typewritten schedule that listed her feeding schedule, the special care she required, and things to watch for. Not only did the sitter have to feed Jenny every three hours, but she also had to keep her gastrostomy tube clean, and every hour she had to moisten her mouth and "let her suck on a wet cloth if she seems thirsty." As the new sitter's eyes moved from the top of the page to the bottom and she flipped the page, her posture would start to sag, and she'd become less talkative. The sitter only needed to let me know if Jenny's eyes rolled back more than normal, but she *did* need to keep an eye out for grand mal seizures. If Jenny's body stiffened and her hands or legs started to shake—and this happened more than one time—the sitter needed to call me *immediately*. Also, if Jenny's breathing seemed more shallow than usual, the sitter needed to shake her and call her name. No worries—her breathing should pick up if she'd do that.

After a few days, I'd pick up Jenny, and the babysitter avoided my eyes. I knew what was coming. She'd inevitably shuffle her feet, bite her lip, and stammer.

"I'm really sorry—she's such a sweetheart." She'd give Jenny a tender look and smile before she continued. "—but I don't think this is going to work out." She'd then look everywhere except at me.

I'd mumble something like "That's okay" or "I understand," and I'd tote Jenny to the car and get her situated in her travel chair.

That night, I'd call Fern because sometimes she would fill in between babysitters. If Fern said, "No," Allan and I took turns taking off work until we found another babysitter.

# CHAPTER TWENTY-NINE

It was cloudy all day on Friday, September 12, and the fifty-degree morning temperatures made the whole apartment feel chilly and drab. Jenny had a temperature of 105 degrees.

At 7:00 a.m., I picked up the receiver and dialed Cessna. After I left a message for Myrna, I reached inside the white-metal kitchen cabinet and pulled out a bottle of Tylenol. I crushed it and sprinkled it into Jenny's formula container. I shook the thermometer down again at noon and inserted it ever so slightly into Jenny's Vaseline-covered rectum. When I pulled it out and read it, my eyes widened, and I rubbed my chin. The red-mercury line touched 105 degrees. My thoughts swirled as if trying to understand. *Jenny's temperature always goes down when I give her Tylenol.*

I sat on the edge of the double bed and dialed Dr. Robinson's office. The receptionist put me on hold, so I sat in a slouched position and waited—and waited. When I heard the clacking of the receiver being picked up, I sat up straight and listened. "Dr. Robinson says to wait, and if she's still running a temperature in the morning, you should take her to the hospital."

All that day, the sky was gray. The outside temperature never got over sixty-eight degrees, and Jenny's temperature never fell below 105 degrees. By midnight, Allan and I were drained, so we made an agreement. Allan would stay up with Jenny until 3:00 a.m., and we would switch: he would sleep, and I would stay up with Jenny from 3:00 to 6:00 a.m. At 3:00 a.m., I felt the bedspread move, and Allan lay down. "Her breathing is stable—I don't think you need to get up." I slept for the next three hours.

At 6:00 a.m. I woke up suddenly and turned the switch on the lamp that sat on the bedside table. I leaped out of bed and took the one step to Jenny's white crib. Jenny lay on her stomach with a pillow situated under her hips, so she was in a reclined position with her head down. Her face was turned toward our double bed, and her light brown hair flowed across the white sheet. The first thing I noticed was that a puddle of dark liquid had drooled out of her mouth. My chest tightened at the thought as to why this happened. I reached my hand inside her crib and rested my hand on her back. I couldn't feel any rhythmic breathing. My chest tightened more, and I backed away from the crib. *Her head should have been tilted up—not down. Could she have choked on the fluid?*

My voice felt hysterical. "I don't feel her breathing!" Allan threw back the bedspread and lifted her out of the crib as I took another step back and out of the way. For the first time, I couldn't go near her—I couldn't touch her. Allan sat back down on the edge of the double bed and arranged Jenny on his lap. He held Jenny on his lap and felt her body for signs of life.

He perked up and made strong eye contact with me. "I feel a pulse!" We both threw on clothes and raced to the Torino. Allan sat in the passenger seat with Jenny on his lap, and I got in the driver's seat. I ran through stop signs and stop lights, wheeled up to the door of the emergency room, and left the car in front of the door.

◆ ◆ ◆

The emergency room was quiet, cold, and sterile. Empty plastic chairs lined the white walls of the waiting room. A middle-aged, light-brown-haired receptionist with reading glasses glanced up when we rushed into the room. With a stone face, she reached for the standard medical forms. I followed after Allan when he rushed toward the door of the clinic, but the receptionist held out her hand. "Wait a minute! You'll have to check in before you go back."

Jenny lay limp in Allan's arms, and I watched him push through the door. I stepped in front of the glass that separated me and the receptionist and waited for her to gather her papers. "What is the full name of the patient?" I rocked in place and rubbed my arms as I glanced back and forth between the door Jenny had just gone through and the face of this soulless woman. "Who is the responsible party?" She leisurely dawdled the answer to each question before she asked the next one. "What's the name of your insurance company?"

After an eternity, she finally tapped the papers on the counter and excused me. I lurched toward the door. On the other side of the door, a white-capped nurse pointed to a room. I recalled the time Jenny's lips had turned blue and the babysitter had rushed her to the emergency room. I expected to find Jenny surrounded by doctors and nurses who bustled around her. I stepped up to the door and stopped. I couldn't go in. There were no nurses—or doctors; in fact, there was no movement of any kind. Allan stood alongside the hospital bed and faced the doorway. Jenny lay across the hospital bed behind him. Neither of them moved. Sadness clouded Allan's face.

"Jackie, she's not alive." I stared at him with an unfocused gaze. My mind raced back to the puddle of dark liquid that had come out of Jenny's mouth, and I remembered that her head had been down. *She must not have been able to breathe!* I thought. My face contorted.

"It's my fault—I killed her!" The nurse jerked her head. Hot tears streamed down my face, and my voice sounded hysterical. "Jenny's head was down, and it should have been up!" My head swung toward the nurse. "Please call Dr. Robinson." The nurse nodded and led us down the hall. I had a tightness in my chest that wouldn't go away, and I couldn't talk. People around me bustled down the hall, and excited sounds came out when their lips moved, but I couldn't hear or comprehend anything. She guided us into a small room that was set up like a living room. A box of Kleenex sat on the end table beside a lamp and a black rotary desk phone. "You can make calls from here." She closed the door softly behind her, and Allan and I sat in silence. Eventually, I reached for the receiver on the black phone while Allan went back to the emergency room entrance to park the car.

After I called my dad and Aunt Lee, Dr. Robinson came into the room with the nurse who had led us down the hall. With red-raw eyes and trembling lips, I told him that Jenny's head was down, and I should have had it propped up. Dr. Robinson shook his head vigorously. "No—that had absolutely nothing to do with it. None of this is your fault." I noticed him eyeing the nurse to make sure she understood.

◆ ◆ ◆

Aunt Lee knocked gently on the waiting room door, and Allan opened it. Her head tilted to the side, and she gave me a pained glance. When she sat down beside me, she patted my knee. After some useless chitchat, Aunt Lee began to take control.

"I think it would be better if you came and stayed with me for a few days."

"Why?"

"I think it would be too hard for you to go back to your apartment right now."

"Why?"

"Well—I—I think it would be better for you emotionally."

I had no idea what she was talking about. With a heavy heart, I slipped into a black hole I had never known before. I would do whatever she wanted.

Later that morning on Saturday, September 13, Allan and I strode out of the visitor's room, and we pushed through the hospital's glass door and into the parking lot. I opened the door of the Torino, scooted into the passenger seat, and lit another cigarette. It was overcast and sixty degrees. We pulled up to the exit of the hospital and watched cars zoom down the street. I took a drag of my cigarette and flipped the ashes out the window. Allan and I sat in silence. At age twenty-five, the reality of death was completely foreign to me. I watched cars fly by.

"How do people continue with their lives as if nothing happened?" I slumped slightly forward and rubbed my eyelids. "How can everything just go on as usual?"

Allan took a drag of his cigarette and shook his head. "I have no idea." When the traffic stopped, he crept out into the street and headed to Aunt Lee's house.

# CHAPTER THIRTY

It was a cool, cloudy day when Aunt Lee drove me to Old Mission Cemetery that afternoon. I stared at the sidewalk as we strolled up to the door of a huge, gray-brick building. A gray-haired man led us into a private room, and we settled into the two chairs that faced his huge wooden desk. We all lit up cigarettes, and the cemetery guy pulled forms out of his desk. My head went back and forth between the gray-haired man and Aunt Lee.

"We need a plot for a little girl," Aunt Lee said.

"How old?"

Aunt Lee looked at me. "She's three, isn't she?" I nodded.

He took a deep drag off his cigarette and set it back in the ashtray. "Well, she's too big to be buried in Babyland." He reached for a pencil and circled rectangular shapes on his map. "Do you want a vault?" I frowned and glanced toward Aunt Lee.

She veered her eyes toward the gray-haired man. "What's a vault?"

"It's a cement container that the casket goes in," he said.

"Why?" I asked.

"To protect the casket from water and anything else that might seep into it."

"Yes." I leaned toward his desk and flicked my ashes. "I definitely want a vault."

"It will cost more."

"That's OK." I leaned back in the chair, and with my lips pressed together, I looked him squarely in the eyes. The cemetery guy nodded and scribbled on the order form.

We all stood up and sauntered out into the cemetery. We strolled through grass that provided a platform for perfectly aligned upright granite headstones and rectangular-shaped granite blocks with names and dates.

The man wandered up to an empty plot that was situated under a tree. "This is nice," Aunt Lee said.

I looked up at the leaves that were beginning to turn red and gold. "Yes, it would be nice having her here." I scanned the area and noticed a white cement bench close by. "Yeah—this will work."

As we trekked back to the gray building, my eyes were drawn to a granite stone with an oval picture of the person on the corner of the smooth, slate stone.

"I want Jenny's picture on her stone."

"You'll design the headstone later, but putting her picture on it will cost quite a bit more," said the gray-haired man.

I furrowed my brow and sighed dejectedly. "That doesn't matter."

✦ ✦ ✦

While Aunt Lee and I were at Old Mission Cemetery, Uncle Gilbert and Allan drove up to Downing East Funeral Home. When the funeral home owner agreed to let us make payments, Allan took a step back and became speechless. Who gives credit to a young couple steeped in debt for medical bills and—now—funeral bills? Then, Allan noticed the huge smile plastered on Uncle Gilbert's face and the friendly camaraderie between him and the owner. After an hour of negotiating money and funeral payments, Allan shook the owner's hand, climbed into Uncle Gilbert's car, and headed to Old Mission Cemetery.

✦ ✦ ✦

At Old Mission Cemetery, it was a different story. Both Uncle Gilbert and Allan sat in front of the same gray-haired man who had talked with Aunt Lee and me earlier that day. This time, though, the discussion evolved around the cost and how to pay for all the arrangements Aunt Lee and I had made.

"You'll have to pay upfront for the burial plot," said the gray-haired man. He snuffed out a cigarette butt, leaned back into his swivel chair, and folded his hands behind his head. "You'll have to pay cash for that."

Allan's knee started to bounce, and he cleared his throat. "When do I need to get the money to you?"

"I'm sorry, but we can't bury her until we have the $350."

Allan made the dreaded phone call to his dad, and later that day, he handed $350 to the gray-haired cemetery guy.

◆ ◆ ◆

Sunday evening, Allan drove me to the funeral home. He opened the door for me, and we tiptoed in. The scent of fresh flowers permeated throughout the large, carpeted room. Along the sides of the room were sofas and winged-back chairs in soft, pastel colors. Polished wooden coffee tables and end tables held shaded lamps that cast a soft glow. Beside each bell-shaped lamp was a box of Kleenex. There was no sound and no movement. A middle-aged man must have heard the door open because he appeared out of nowhere. He seemed to know who we wanted to see, and he led us to a room with white double doors. He spread out the doors and waved toward her casket. Then, he disappeared. I stood at the door. Jenny's light-pink casket sat on a white table, and her head lay on a white-satin pillow. She was surrounded by white-satin fluffs. Allan pushed the middle of my back toward the casket. I took a couple of small steps forward. The tightness in my chest would not loosen, and I had no strength.

"I'll leave you alone." Allan took two steps back and closed the doors behind me.

Eventually, I dragged my feet toward her casket. I felt an ache in my throat that went up through the back of my eyes until they filled with tears. I stood over Jenny and gazed down at her. *Why are her lips together?* I thought. Jenny's mouth was always open. *Oh, they sewed her mouth together.* My eyes roamed over her light-brown hair and pastel-pink dress with gathers and lace. My fingers trembled as I reached out to touch her cheek, but she felt cold and hard. I pulled my hand back. A few moments later, I tried again. I reached for her hand, and it wasn't as difficult this time. I lifted Jenny's hand, but it was so hard and cold. I put my right hand under her small hand and my left hand on top of her cold hand and pressed them together to try to warm her. I reached for her arms and tried to warm them up too. My fear began to evaporate. I ran my fingers over the folds and lace on her dress. I dug through my purse for a comb and found one at the very bottom. I slowly dragged the comb through her hair and shaped her hair just so around her face. Then, I combed through her bangs to make them look the way they were supposed to. I straightened out her dress and all the satin that surrounded her. I fiddled with Jenny and stayed with her by myself for who knows how long. Finally, I bent down, kissed her, and turned toward the white double doors.

When I opened them, Allan's eyes widened. He was sprawled across one of the wing-backed chairs, and when he saw me, he jumped up, planted his feet on the carpet, and stood up. On the end table beside him, a lit cigarette sat on the edge of a glass ashtray full of cigarette butts.

"Ready?"

I picked up his lit cigarette, took a couple of drags, and crushed it out. "Yeah."

♦ ♦ ♦

Jenny died on Saturday, September 13, and her funeral was at 11:00 a.m. on Monday, September 15. Jenny's casket was open at the front of the room, and the immediate family was off to the side behind a designated closed-curtained area. Even though it was fifty-five degrees outside and overcast, I wore a light pastel-pink dress to her funeral. I didn't notice that everyone else wore black. I stared down at my hands and felt the familiar tightness in my chest. When the pastor gave the eulogy, I didn't hear anything he said. I just wanted to get out of there and be left alone. After it was over, everyone drove to the gravesite. I sat in a folded chair in front of Jenny's casket, and as soon as the pastor stopped talking, I stood up and wandered toward the waiting car without saying a word to anyone. I didn't know the protocol, and I didn't care.

✦ ✦ ✦

At Uncle Gilbert's house, the aroma of freshly baked rolls and roast mingled with the noisy chatter of cousins and family who had not seen each other in years. The solemnness of the funeral was over, and everyone laughed at each other's jokes as they passed around mashed potatoes. When I couldn't stand it anymore, I got up from the table and strode out of the dining room, through the living room, past the black Steinway, up the elegant wooden staircase, and into my cousin's bedroom. The bedroom walls were covered with light-pink paint, and I immediately fell onto the ruffled bedspread, turned on my side, and stared into the attached pink-tiled bathroom with a black tub and black sink. Finally—quiet.

A few minutes later, Allan and my dad knocked softly on the bedroom door before they cracked it open and saw me. There was nothing to say.

"Why don't you come to Virginia for a couple of weeks?" my dad said. I turned on my back and stared at the ceiling. The thought of running away gave me a glimmer of hope that maybe I could find some sort of relief from this unrelenting pain in my chest and overwhelming fatigue.

"Maybe."

An hour later, I lifted myself from that bed, and I followed my dad and Allan to whatever was next.

# CHAPTER THIRTY-ONE

I found that everything that had been familiar all of a sudden became new and unfamiliar. Everything was a first. The first time I went to the grocery store—the first time I went to the bank—or the first time I did any other mundane task of life, I had to learn to do it without having Jenny in my life. The first time I entered my apartment was the worst.

Allan jiggled the key into the keyhole and stepped aside to let me enter first. I inched through the door, and I didn't recognize it. Fresh flowers from the funeral home were set here and there, but there was no travel chair in the living room, no baby food in the kitchen cabinets, no white crib in the bedroom, and none of Jenny's clothes were in the closet or the chest of drawers. With dark circles under my eyes and no energy, I let my purse fall off my shoulder and onto the floor. I dragged myself back to the bedroom, sprawled out on top of my double bed, and closed my eyes.

❖ ❖ ❖

The following Thursday, my mom left, so Allan and I got into the Torino, and he drove to my dad's house in Virginia while I slept. Dad had divorced my mom and was living with his secretary, who was three years older than I was. His house smelled of new construction and happiness. Dad tiptoed around me and always asked me questions: "Can I get you anything? Are you sure you're comfortable? Do you feel like eating?" I just wanted to sleep while they wanted to move on and start living again.

Allan left me sleeping in the guest room and headed toward the bedroom door. He flipped off the light switch and skipped down the stairs. The family room was filled with the smell of cigarette smoke, pizza, and alcohol. Aunt Lee happened to be visiting my dad, her older brother, so Allan was able to mingle with people who gave him a reprieve from my somberness. Dad laid pepperoni pizza across the kitchen counter and pulled a beer out of the refrigerator while Aunt Lee poured scotch and water for herself.

"What do you drink, Allan?"

"Scotch and water."

Aunt Lee lit up. "That's my kind of guy!"

The Clark family was quick-witted, so the jokes flew, and the chuckles turned to laughter. The laughter grew louder with each refill of scotch and water. Eventually, the laughter weaved its way up to the bedroom, so I gathered the strength to get up and stumble down the stairs. With sleep lines on my face and dark circles under my eyes, I crawled into a chair in the corner of the room and lit a cigarette.

My dad came over and patted me on the leg. "Want some pizza?" I shook my head.

They resumed their reveling, and I watched Aunt Lee refill Allan's glass of scotch and water. After the third refill, my mind wandered to scenes from my childhood and my sister talking to me in the bathroom. *Mom only loves people when she's drunk.* I rubbed my hand over my belly. I flew out of my seat and marched toward Allan. "I need to talk to you." I kept marching until we were out of earshot.

"What—what's the matter?" Allan rubbed his chin and swallowed.

"You're drinking!" My eyes were cold and hard.

Allan glanced down at the drink in his hand and back at me. "So?" His eyebrows squished together in confusion.

"My mom was an alcoholic, and there's no way in hell I'm going to raise my baby with an alcoholic father."

"Oh." A slow smile crept across his face. Allan set the drink on a nearby table. "No problem."

When we drove back to Wichita, I noticed that the trip had given me no relief at all.

◆ ◆ ◆

After two weeks, we both had to go back to work. I stepped up the stairs at Cessna for the first time since Jenny died, and I wandered down the hall to my office. I sat at my desk that overlooked the shop, and I noticed Maxine watching me. I met her eyes.

"I'm so—I'm so sorry" was all she could say before her eyes welled up, and she looked away.

I could feel tears begin to fill my eyes, so I murmured a quick "Thanks," uncovered my typewriter, and started sorting papers.

Every evening after work, Allan and I would drive home, and I would lie down on the navy-blue, floral sofa. If Allan tried to show affection, I pushed him away. I'd never known permanency before—and I found that death was permanent. I couldn't see how I would *ever* find any hope or relief from this constant tightness in my chest and this black hole I lived in.

◆ ◆ ◆

Buried in a stack of sympathy cards, I noticed a letter from Eva Mae, my religious aunt in California. I lit a cigarette and settled back into the navy sofa. I tore the envelope and pulled out two pages of cream-colored stationary with black cursive writing on them. I started reading.

"Dear Jackie, the most wonderful thing in the world to know is that the Lord doeth all things well." *She means well,* I thought. I continued to read sentences such as "Wasn't it wonderful that He loaned her to you for a while here?" and "… look how much sweeter heaven is now because she is there." I threw my head back on the navy-flowered sofa cushion, took a deep breath, and felt my eyes tighten. *This is torture,* I thought. After the short mental reprieve, I lifted my head, took a drag off my cigarette, and continued reading.

"David lost a child and in II Samuel 12:23 we read, 'I shall go to him, but he shall not return to me.'" I stopped and could feel my posture stiffen. I returned to the letter and read the words again. "I shall go to him, but he shall not return to me." I raised my head and stared off into nothing. *Jenny will not come back to me, but I must go to her—I must go to her.*

# CHAPTER THIRTY-TWO

People who knew how to go to heaven went to church, but I sure didn't want to go to the First Evangelical Free Church that Eva Mae recommended because my whole family knew she was a religious nut. So, the United Methodist Church sounded promising. On a beautiful Sunday morning, it was seventy degrees and sunny. Allan and I flipped cigarettes onto the lawn before climbing the cement stairs that led into a huge red-brick building. We entered a grand foyer and traipsed across shiny parquet flooring that flowed into the nave. In the center of the front wall of the sanctuary, a sizable stained-glass window reached almost to the ceiling. A picture of Jesus with stretched-out arms on a cross and surrounded by angels was etched in various colors of red, blue, green, and yellow glass. A few feet in front of the stained-glass window stood an oversized dark-wood podium that was situated in the center of a raised platform. A thin blond woman played somber religious songs on the organ in the left-hand corner while church attendees found their seats among rows of dark-wood pews. Wooden holders behind each pew held hard-back hymnals. It was an older building, so a musty scent pooled with the smell of soap and cologne. Men in suits and ties and women in their Sunday dresses slid into pews and pulled out hymnals.

Allan and I scooted into one of the pews toward the back and followed the lead of those around us. We opened our hymnals to page fifty-six, stood, and sang. After a couple of songs, we all sat down and bowed our heads. Then, we sang another three songs before everyone shut their hymnals, put them back into the wooden cubby hole, and looked to the front of the church in anticipation. An elderly, gray-headed man strolled to the front and stood behind the podium. I leaned forward in hopes that this man would explain *exactly* how to get to heaven. Nothing he said even sounded religious. Periodically, he would mention God, but we had no idea what he was talking about. At one point, the minister wandered to the right side of the platform and stood in front of some sort of map. He invited elementary school children to come to the front of the sanctuary. Boys and girls giggled as they formed a semicircle around the colored map he had propped up on some sort of stand. He told the children that the map shows us how to get from one place to another. He used a pointer to point to an area on one side of the map and then moved it to another area of the map. Allan and I shook our heads slightly as we glanced at each other and frowned.

After the service, everyone closed their eyes and prayed. When we opened them, the minister had magically disappeared from the raised platform and now stood at the back of the church ready to shake hands. When it was our turn to shake the minister's hand, I gathered the courage to ask my question. The minister beamed as he held out his hand to me.

"I'm interested in how to get to heaven," I said as I clasped his hand.

The minister's head flinched back slightly. "That's a good question." His gaze clouded over, and he ran his hands through his hair.

I stood there for a moment in anticipation. Allan finally broke the awkward silence and shook his hand. He pushed the middle of my back to guide me out the door.

◆ ◆ ◆

I'd spent hours at the dinette table designing Jenny's grave marker, and I finally finished it. Old Mission Cemetery recommended that we go to Quiring Monument to have it made. The blond-headed receptionist at Quiring led us to a private room and pointed to a couple of chairs in front of a dark-wood desk. On top of the desk were a couple of ashtrays, a container that held several pens, and a calculator. Allan pulled a couple of cigarettes out of his shirt pocket and handed one to me. He flicked his Bic lighter and lit my cigarette before lighting his. A few minutes later, a middle-aged, black-haired representative of Quiring Monument came through the door and situated himself in the chair behind the desk. After he pulled a couple of forms out of his desk, he intertwined his fingers, placed his hands on the desk, and leaned toward us.

"How can we help?"

FOR THE LOVE OF GOD

"We need a flat grave marker," I said as I pulled a sheet of paper out of my purse and smoothed it out in front of him with the lettering facing him. I pointed to each item as I explained. "On the far-left side, I want a cross with a rose draped over the top of it carved into the stone." I used a pen from the container as a pointer and dragged it from the bottom of the rose to the top. I moved the pen to the middle of the paper. "In the middle and on the top line, I want the words 'God's Very Special Child,' and on the second line, I want the words 'My Beloved Daughter.'" I continued to lean over the drawing and point to each line.

The man stared at my drawing and nodded his head as he periodically stopped to take notes. "Right under that, I want the word *Jenny* on a line by itself." Allan rubbed his hand down his pant leg as he watched the man's expression. "Then, I want her full name, birth date, and death date right here." After a final tap on the sheet, I put the pen back inside the container and took a drag of my cigarette.

The black-haired man rubbed his chin and pointed to the upper right-hand corner of my drawing. "What's this oval?"

"That's where I want her picture." I dug into my purse and handed him Jenny's picture. "I want it in color."

The man held the picture, nodded, and gave a deep sigh. He laid the picture on top of the form where he had made a list. With his left finger, he went down the list, and with his right hand, he clicked numbers on the calculator. Allan's knee began to bounce.

"You know that the special details and picture add a considerable amount to the cost."

"Yeah—I know." I crossed my arms and waited.

When the black-haired man stopped clicking on the calculator, he turned to us. "The average cost of a flat grave marker is around \$250, but with your added details and colored ceramic picture, it will cost \$600."

I noticed that Allan's leg stopped bouncing, and he went completely still. The black-haired man noticed it too. "You can arrange to make payments if you need to."

My eyes swung from Allan to the man sitting on the other side of the desk. I pushed my shoulders back and sat up straight. "Yes—we'll do that."

# CHAPTER THIRTY-THREE

I first learned to drive a stick shift in Allan's brand-new red Pacer. I'd drive around with my head ducked down, and if someone pulled up beside me, I'd stare straight ahead and feel my cheeks flush. After a while, I stopped at a stoplight and glanced at the guy who pulled up next to me. The guy didn't notice me or shake his head in disgust at the weird car, but he leaned forward and smiled and nodded as he scrutinized the Pacer. After that, I held my head up when I drove the Pacer, and I was no longer surprised at the glances and questions.

Allan's eyebrows would pinch together, and he'd shake his head when he wrote the check for the payment on the Pacer.

"With all the medical and funeral bills, we need to get out from under this car payment," he said. I muttered something about him doing whatever he wanted.

So, after work one cloudy evening in the middle of October, we put on our jackets, and I followed Allan to his parents' house. I parked my Torino in front of their green and white three-bedroom, one-bath home as Allan pulled his Pacer onto their single-car driveway. He turned off the ignition and just sat there staring at his hands with his fingers wrapped around the steering wheel. His dad peered through the picture window in the living room, and when he saw the Pacer, the curtain swung back to its usual position.

He trotted out the front door onto the rectangular-shaped cement porch that held two white-metal chairs with a small white-metal table between them and an ashtray on top. Allan's dad gave a glance and quick wave toward my Torino before he turned his attention to the car in the driveway. By this time, Allan stood beside the car and leaned against the passenger door as he inhaled several drags of his cigarette. With slumped shoulders and dull eyes, he watched his dad meander around the Pacer and stop periodically to rub his finger over imagined imperfections. After a few moments, he stopped beside Allan with a nod and a satisfied smile. Allan straightened up and handed his dad the keys and the payment book. Within five minutes, the red Pacer—and the car payment—were gone.

◆ ◆ ◆

Every day, Allan and I would leave Cessna and go to the cemetery. It was the end of October, so the leaves were gold and red, and the weather was breezy and sixty degrees. Allan climbed into the driver's seat while I clambered into the passenger's seat and slammed the door. As Allan pulled out of the Cessna parking lot, he leaned to the side and reached in his jacket pocket for a pack of cigarettes.

"I have to get flowers," I said.

Allan's head turned to me, and there was a visible tightness in his jaw and neck. "We just bought flowers." I ignored him.

Allan pulled into the parking lot of Wall's IGA, and a few minutes later, I came back with a planter that held an arrangement of fall flowers. I held the flowers on my lap as he pulled out of the parking lot and steered toward the cemetery.

"How much?"

"Five dollars."

He seemed to struggle to find the right words. "I understand you want fresh flowers for Jenny's grave."

"That's right—I do." I lit a cigarette and blew smoke out of the corner of my mouth.

Allan tilted his head in a side-to-side rhythm. "We just can't afford it."

My eyes narrowed, my face reddened, and I turned and faced him. "You can't tell me what I can and can't do." Allan's fingers tightened around the steering wheel, and he shook his head as his lips curled.

"Why in the hell don't you understand that we don't have the money for this?"

I took a deep drag off my cigarette and put it in the ashtray before I turned to him.

"Why don't *you* understand that you can go straight to hell?!" I rolled down the window with my right hand then pulled the diamond ring off my finger on my left hand. With a sweep of my right arm, I threw the ring out the window as far as I could.

Allan slammed on the brakes, and we both flew forward. He

FOR THE LOVE OF GOD

pounded the palms of his hands on the steering wheel and turned toward me with bulging eyes and heavy breathing. My eyes bore into his—and there was silence. After a moment, his body began to lose its tenseness, and he climbed out of the car. With his eyes bent down close to the ground, he wandered up and down the grassy area near the narrow road that wound through the cemetery. It never entered my mind that the diamond ring was the only thing we owned that was worth anything—but he knew it.

I stepped out of the car and made the familiar trip to Jenny's grave. I picked up the dying flowers and replaced them with a planter full of fall flowers. A cold breeze swept over me, and my eyebrows drew together as I stooped over her grave. *Oh gosh, she'll get cold when it starts to freeze!*

+ + +

I finally succumbed to the idea of visiting the church Eva Mae had recommended—the First Evangelical Free Church. At 10:30 on Sunday morning, we drove down Woodlawn to the red-brick building that spread out every which way, and on the roof in the middle of the building stood a pointed fixture that reached the sky and was topped with a cross. We entered a modern foyer, picked up a leaflet, and traipsed into the nave. There were no stained-glass windows or an elaborate podium in the sanctuary in front of the church; however, there was a sort of clean, gentle smell and a simple podium that stood in the center. The wall that faced the congregation held a sizeable lighted cross. Off to the side, a short-haired woman sat behind a piano and gently pressed keys so soft music welcomed all the familiar churchgoers. The wall-to-wall, soft-beige Berber carpet contrasted with the rows of dark wood pews. Behind each pew were the standard hymnal holders that held a couple of red hymnals on each side of a hard-backed Bible. On the side of the holder, there was a slot for a tiny pencil and small visitors' cards. After we settled into the end of one pew, I pulled out a visitor's card and managed to write our name, address, and phone number in the tiny space with the tiny pencil.

The piano music stopped, and a youngish man stepped up on the platform and told us to turn our hymnals to page 163. Again, we sang when we were supposed to sing and bowed our heads when we were supposed to pray. Eventually, the music stopped. The youngish man stepped off the platform, and a thirty-something-year-old, dark-headed man dressed in the typical dark suit, white shirt, and tie strode up to the podium. We were to turn our Bibles to some verse in John. Allan and I picked up a Bible from the holder in front of us and glanced around. Within seconds, everyone had flipped their Bibles to the right place. We looked through the Bible and finally realized that in the front of it was a list of names with page numbers beside them. I ran my index finger down each name until I found the word *John*. We couldn't understand most of what the pastor said, but eventually, he said something I'd never heard before. He said that Jesus was *God*. *Really?* He never did tell us how to get to heaven.

After the pastor closed his Bible, he started rattling on about something called communion. He went on and on about not taking communion unless you knew Jesus as your Lord and Savior. Allan and I looked at each other with confused looks and shrugged our shoulders.

As they passed silver trays with tiny glass cups filled with grape juice and little pieces of crackers to each person, Allan leaned over to me. "I don't think we're supposed to be doing this."

I flipped my hair back over my shoulder and took a glimpse at those around me as I cleared my throat. Allan also glanced around and then shrunk down into his seat. The white-haired lady sitting next to me smiled and handed me the silver tray. To avoid embarrassment, I took one of the tiny glass cups and handed the tray to Allan. He took one, too.

After the drink and cracker trays were stacked on the table in front of the sanctuary, they passed around a basket for money. I dug through my purse for a dollar and tossed it in the basket along with the white visitor's card.

# CHAPTER THIRTY-FOUR

The next day, Allan said a guy from the church called and wanted to come see us. My face lit up. "What'd you tell him?"

"I said that would be fine, and he said he'd be here tomorrow night at 6:30 or so."

"Oh gosh." I bit my lip and pinched the skin on my throat. I opened the white-metal kitchen cabinets for some sort of snack and the refrigerator for some sort of drink to serve this guy. The cabinets were empty, so we climbed into the Torino and drove to Walls IGA.

The next evening, the apartment smelled of popcorn, and glasses of iced Coke sat on the coffee table in front of the navy sofa. The sky was overcast with a gentle breeze, and the temperature was sixty-two degrees when Allan opened the front door and stepped onto the small square cement porch. His head turned this way and that as his eyes darted up and down Hunter Street.

I cracked open the front door. "Why in the world are you standing on the front porch?"

Allan glanced back at me over his shoulder. "I want to be sure they find us."

I shook my head slightly and stepped back into the living room to make sure everything was just right. At 6:35, a car with two men pulled up in front of the apartment, and Allan waved and grinned. An older man opened the driver's side door, and a younger man opened the door on the passenger side. The older man was fortyish with graying hair and wire-rimmed glasses, and the younger, black-haired man was in his middle twenties and wore black, horn-rimmed glasses. With Bibles under their arms, both men marched up the sidewalk to our front door. The older man's eyes sparkled, and he gave us a wide grin as he stretched out his hand. The younger man gave us a forced smile as his eyes wandered over each piece of furniture in our apartment. The older man sat on the navy chair while the younger man sat on a kitchen chair that I had dragged in from under the wooden dinette table. As soon as I realized there were *two* men, I bounced toward the kitchen for another glass, filled it with ice and Coke, and set it on the coffee table in front of the younger man. He nodded, took his first gulp, and reached for a handful of popcorn.

They both sat across from us on the opposite side of the coffee table, and Allan and I leaned back and settled into the navy sofa. The older man took control of the conversation.

"How did you happen to find our church?"

"I have an aunt who recommended it," I said.

"Oh—does she live around here?"

"No, she lives in California."

The older man's head flinched back slightly, and his forehead furrowed. "California?"

Allan sat up straight and used hand gestures as he explained the whole situation about Jenny and the letter Eva Mae had sent. Allan stopped talking, and there was silence. Before the silence got awkward, I spoke up.

"So, what we *really* want to know is how do we get to heaven?" That being said, we both leaned back on the navy-flowered cushions and waited for the older man to give us some answers. Instead, he asked Allan a question.

"If you were standing at the gates of heaven and God asked you why He should let you in, what would you say?"

Allan sat there with a clouded gaze and stared off into nowhere. "Well—let me think." He hung his head and finally let out a hard sigh. "If God were to ask me that, I guess I would think He wasn't going to let me in." Allan's body began to shrink.

The older man's half-smile turned into a wide, toothy grin. "That's right!"

My eyes went back and forth from Allan to the older man as each one spoke. Something was going on, but I just sat there with a confused look on my face.

The older man started talking about sin and Jesus and how he needed to ask Jesus into his heart—the same ole thing I'd heard Eva Mae chatter about almost two years ago. But for some reason, Allan kept steady eye contact with the older man and nodded his head in agreement. Something was happening, but it sure didn't involve me.

*Why is all this so new to you?* I thought. *Surely, you've heard it all before.*

"Would you like to pray?" the older man said.

Allan nodded, propped his forearms on his knees, and laced his fingers together. After everyone had bowed their heads, the older man guided Allan through a prayer about sin, forgiveness, and giving his life to Jesus. Allan repeated every word.

Before the two guys left, the older one pulled a set of small cards out of his pocket.

"Here are some verses you might want to memorize." He laid the small stack of verse cards on the coffee table. Allan and I glanced down at the cards in confusion. "It's really good to get in the habit of memorizing." We plastered smiles on our faces and escorted the men to the door. After many thanks, handshaking, and slaps on the back, the two guys shuffled down the sidewalk and into their car. Allan and I closed the front door and started picking up empty glasses and popcorn remnants. I picked up the verses. "What should I do with these?"

Allan shrugged his shoulders as he tucked the kitchen chair under the table. "Heck if I know."

"You want me to just throw them away?"

"I guess." We both chuckled as I threw them in the trash.

◆ ◆ ◆

Every evening after we'd get back from the cemetery, I'd drag myself into the apartment that belonged to Jenny and me, lie down on the navy sofa, and sleep. Eventually, the sadness and loneliness became overwhelming, and Allan tapped on my shoulder. "What do you think about moving to another apartment?"

I turned on my back, weaved my fingers through my hair, and tapped my index finger against my lip. "Maybe that's not a bad idea."

My landlady listened in silence and squeezed my hand when I told her I wanted to move out of my apartment and into a two-bedroom. She turned in her chair, reached behind her for a notebook, and scanned through a list of all seventy-five apartment units to check availability. Within a month, Allan and I moved a couple of blocks down the street, around the corner, and into a two-bedroom unit in a blond-brick duplex.

The rent on the two-bedroom apartment was higher than my one-bedroom, but the extra expense wasn't the problem. We still owed thousands of dollars for Jenny's medical and funeral bills. A couple of weeks after we moved into the two-bedroom apartment, Allan got a part-time job. Three times a week, he'd put on a red shirt and wait tables at the nearby Pizza Inn.

# CHAPTER THIRTY-FIVE

Ever since the men from church came to our apartment, Allan seemed more upbeat. His face shined a little more, and he went on and on about his conversation with a couple of religious guys at work. "They were really happy for me when I told them."

I scratched my temple in confusion. None of this made sense. Even though I'd been interested in God for years, I hadn't thought to mention it to coworkers.

Allan continued. "One guy said that he goes to a Bible study in Mulvane, and we could go too—if we wanted."

Later that evening, as usual, I slept on the navy sofa with a blanket pulled up tightly under my chin. Allan was staring at the TV with the volume turned down. When the phone rang, I rolled over and watched Allan traipse back to the bedroom and heard him pick up the avocado receiver. It didn't take long to realize it was the older guy from church.

Allan rambled on about the guys from work and how we might go to a Bible study in Mulvane. Then—he quit talking and listened.

"No, he didn't mention what church he goes to," Allan said. More listening. "Yeah, but Mulvane's not too far."

Fifteen minutes later, Allan placed the receiver back into its holder and strolled back to the living room. "The guy from church wants us to do some sort of Navigator's Bible study with him and his wife."

I turned my head toward him. "You don't want to go to the Bible study with that guy from work?"

"I don't think Henry wants us to go there."

"Henry?"

"Yeah—remember? That's the name of the older guy that came over." Allan's gaze seemed to go distant as he touched the base of his neck. Then, he shrugged and his eyes peered down at me. "He wants us to go to his house every week."

"Really?" I stretched as I turned on my back, threw my arms up over my head, and watched Allan.

He seemed fidgety and kept talking. "Oh—when I told him we were reading the Bible, he said we should get something easier to read than that big blue Bible you got from your aunt." Years ago, Eva Mae had given me a blue Scofield Study Bible. Allan planted himself by my feet at the end of the sofa and lit a cigarette. "Henry said something about getting some Bible called *Good News for Modern Man*."

I nodded my head and stared at him for a few moments. Then, I turned toward the back of the navy sofa and wrapped the blanket back over my shoulder and under my chin. "That's fine."

◆ ◆ ◆

A couple of weeks later, we drove up to Henry's house and climbed out of the Torino with Bibles tucked under our arms. We flipped our cigarettes into the yard before we knocked on his door at 7:00 on Thursday night. Henry's three-bedroom, two-bath house felt toasty compared to the windy, fifty-degree weather outside. The kitchen smelled of left-over dinner, and we noticed two preteen girls peek around the corner. His blond, middle-aged wife, Jan, told them to "get to bed!" We were seated around a wooden kitchen table that was surrounded by four wooden chairs and situated directly under a gold and brown patterned lighting fixture. In front of each chair was a colorful booklet of black, red, and orange with large white lettering that read "Knowing Jesus Christ: Book One of the Studies in Christian Living." After we settled in with glasses of iced tea in front of us, Jan hurried in and abruptly seated herself at one end of the table. After some awkward chitchat, I brought up Jenny.

"What was wrong with her?" She propped her elbow on top of the table, rested her chin on top of her fist, and leaned toward me. Her blue eyes scrutinized my face.

"They said she was profoundly brain damaged, but they didn't really know why." She gave understanding nods as I reminisced.

Henry smiled, fidgeted, and tapped his foot, but he remained silent. After a couple of minutes, he interrupted and changed the subject. "Ready to get started?" I raised my eyebrows and gave him a glassy stare, but his eyes were on Allan.

We followed Henry's lead. When he prayed, we all bowed our heads, and when he opened the booklet to the first lesson, we opened our booklets to the first lesson titled "Jesus Christ is God."

"I didn't know Jesus was God until your pastor mentioned it in church," I said.

Henry's posture stiffened, and he gave me an incredulous stare. "Really?"

I leaned back in my chair and crossed my arms. "Nope. I've never heard *anyone* say Jesus is God."

His eyebrows drew together, and he tilted his head. It seemed as if he started to say something, but he closed his mouth and turned back to the study.

Henry had us take turns reading the question and then we would all turn to the chapter and verse in the Bible. Again, Allan and I turned to the table of contents to find the page number of the book of the Bible. Then, we used our index fingers to find the little number that was the verse. While we sluggishly maneuvered our way toward the correct verse, Henry thumbed—ever so slowly—through his own Bible, so we both landed on the verse at the same time.

After we answered the last question in the lesson, he told us that we'd need to have the next lesson done by next week. He closed the booklet and handed Allan and me a small card and a small leather case to put it in.

Allan rubbed his chin. "What's this?"

"This is where you will keep the verses you memorize. The card is your first verse: John 5:24. You have to have it memorized by next Thursday—word for word—no mistakes." The corners of his eyes crinkled. We jerked our heads back and blinked our eyes. *We also have to memorize verses?*

✦ ✦ ✦

Henry and Jan invited us to a Navigator meeting on a Friday night. So, at 6:30 on the appointed Friday night, we smashed out our cigarettes and threw on our coats. With our Bibles tucked under our arms, we stepped out of the apartment and into the windy forty-degree weather and squeezed into the backseat of the couple's green Volkswagen Bug. About thirty minutes later, we pulled up to a sizable house that was well kept—and intimidating. Lines of cars were parked against the curb on each side of the street, so Henry pulled in front of the last parked car.

We rang the doorbell, and a middle-aged, dark-haired woman beamed when she saw Henry and Jan. She escorted us to the family room, and on the way, we passed a dining room table filled with cookies, snacks, and eight-ounce cups stacked and ready to be filled with coffee or tea. The family room had about twelve chairs arranged in a largish circle, and on each chair was a sheet of paper that contained song lyrics. The hostess pointed to the refreshments and swung her hand toward the chairs. "Just choose a seat and grab some snacks." She grinned, turned, and headed toward the kitchen.

Many of the seats had Bibles or coats on them, so we had to find two seats that didn't. We picked up the sheet with song lyrics and sat down. The crowd of people smiled, laughed, chatted, and slapped each other on the back or pressed each other's shoulders. My eyes darted

FOR THE LOVE OF GOD

from one small group to another as I glanced around the room. We decided to leave our Bibles on our chairs and head to the dining room table. On the way, various people introduced themselves and shook our hands. With a wide grin, one white-haired lady approached me and introduced herself.

"So—how did you find out about the Navigators?"

"My husband and I are going through a Navigator Bible study with Henry."

All of a sudden, her whole face lit up as if I were some sort of celebrity. I flinched and plastered a smile on my face.

At 7:00, everyone took their seats and turned to a gray-haired man who appeared to be the leader. After he prayed, he told us to get out our lyric sheet, and within seconds, everyone started singing. My posture stiffened, and I watched in amazement as the roomful of people sang songs about God—on a Friday night, no less! Allan and I looked at each other with wide eyes and raised eyebrows. After three songs, everyone tucked their song sheets under their chairs and picked up their Bibles. The gray-haired man told us to turn to James 4. Within seconds, everyone in the room had their Bibles opened to the correct chapter. Our cheeks flushed as we waded through the Bible, but all eyes were on the gray-haired man.

"If the Bible says that 'friendship with the world is enmity with God,' does that mean we shouldn't have anything to do with the world?"

Everyone had an opinion, and everyone was anxious to express it. In wonderment, I turned my head from this person to that person as they spoke.

Before long, it was 9:00, and everyone stood and reached for their coats that were draped over the backs of their chairs. As we crossed the threshold and toward the door, we approached the gray-haired man and the dark-haired woman as they were saying goodbye to their guests.

With an upturned face and a bubbly voice, the gray-haired man stretched out his hand to us as we moseyed through the door. "We hope you enjoyed this."

"Oh, yeah," Allan said. "It was great!"

Again, we squeezed into the backseat of Henry's green Volkswagen and started home. This Christian world was so different and so new to us. With a soft voice, he conversed with us through his rearview mirror.

"What'd you think?"

Allan sat up straight and his eyes danced. "It was incredible." Through the rearview mirror, I could see Henry's face break into a smile.

I said, "You know—you should tell people about this." I turned and stared out the window. When no one spoke, I glanced back to the rearview mirror.

Henry's eyebrows were squished together, and he rubbed his chin. "What do you mean?"

"I mean, no one knows that people will get together to sing songs and talk about God on a Friday night." I leaned toward the front seat and made thoughtful eye contact with Henry through the rearview mirror. "It's kinda like a secret little meeting that no one knows about." I noticed his head jerk a little. I flopped back into the seat and looked up at the stars.

He glanced at Jan, and they looked at each other with a flat gaze for a few moments before they turned and stared straight ahead in silence.

# CHAPTER THIRTY-SIX

We both bought a copy of *Good News for Modern Man*, and every night, we'd sit on the navy sofa with our eyes glued to every page of this easy-to-read New Testament. On Thursdays at 6:00, we'd climb into the Torino and try to get our weekly verse memorized before we knocked on Henry's door. If I had a question from reading *Good News for Modern Man*, I'd open my Bible and ask about it.

"In John 1:1, why does it say that Christ was *with* God but then it says that He *is* God?"

Henry would give me a genuine smile, and with a soft voice, he answered. "Well, it's hard for us because we are all one person. But God is—really—*three* persons in one Being. He is God the Father, God the Son, and God the Holy Spirit." He relaxed and sat back as he nodded his head with satisfaction.

With my arms crossed and my eyebrows furrowed, I gave him a blank stare. When Henry saw the look on my face, he leaned forward.

"It's hard—but we just have to take it by faith because it's *in the Book!*" After he used those words to describe the Bible, Henry and Allan looked at each other with eyes that danced, and both of them chuckled. I just blinked and bit my lip.

There were three lessons in the first Navigator booklet. Since the verse beside the question would tell us where we could find the answer, I just looked up the verse and copied the words from the Bible, and I'd get the right answer. However, so many questions and answers seemed foreign to me. I'd read, "… for what reason did Jesus tell his disciples he was going to heaven?"[1] After I flipped to the right verse, I'd read, "… to prepare a place for you." I'd write those exact words in the lines of my booklet, and I'd stare off into space and pull on my ear. *Prepare what place? Do we all have little rooms to live in?* The last question in the first book asked, "Do you know you have eternal life?" I wrote "yes" and then I wrote all the words I knew would be the right answer.

❖ ❖ ❖

About six weeks later, we were almost finished with "Book Two," and I had also started reading the Old Testament in my *New American Standard Bible*. I began to understand the connection between Jesus, God, and sin.

At 10:25 on the first Sunday in December, Allan parked the car at the back of the church parking lot because we needed to finish our

---

[1] "Knowing Jesus Christ," *Book One of the Studies in Christian Living*. (Colorado Springs: NavPress, 1964), 11.

cigarettes. I took my last drag and smashed it out in the car ashtray. Then, I got out the wet washcloth that was wrapped in Saran Wrap. I unwrapped it, rubbed the washcloth over both my hands, and handed it to Allan to do the same. Then, I'd dig through my purse and pull out a white packet of Wrigley's Spearmint gum. I handed Allan a stick, and we'd both pop the gum in our mouths before we scrambled out of the car and into the frigid thirty-two-degree weather.

After a few "hellos," we found a seat on a wooden pew, took off our coats, and settled in. In the corner of the sanctuary stood a huge Christmas tree that glistened with lights and decorations. As I scanned the room, I noticed a vast number of poinsettias and other Christmas garnishes placed here and there around the church.

The youngish man stepped up to the podium and told us to turn to page 235 and sing "Hark! The Herald Angels Sing." I loved Christmas songs, and I knew every one of them. He raised his hands, and everyone belted out the familiar words—but this time it was different. When I sang the words "Peace on earth, and mercy mild, God and sinners reconciled," my body froze. I stopped singing and reread the words. *God and sinners reconciled,* and my eyes widened. I knew what that meant. We were then told to turn to page 250 and sing "O Come All Ye Faithful." As we sang, I started to pay attention to the words. "Jesus, to Thee be all glory giv'n! Word of the Father, now in flesh appearing!" I stopped again and reread the words. *This means that God came to earth in the flesh.* When we finished singing and everyone sat down, I turned back to the pages and reread the words to the once-familiar Christmas songs. When I read the last stanza of "The First Noel": "... And with His blood / Mankind hath bought,"

I understood what it meant! I closed the hymnal and celebrated Christmas—for the first time.

◆ ◆ ◆

We bought a used crib for five dollars. Allan worked on weekends brushing white paint over both the crib and the used chest of drawers. Since we wouldn't know the sex of the baby until it was born, I couldn't use blue or pink as accent colors, so I bought a yellow-clown lamp and yellow decals from TG&Y and stuck them on the ends of the crib and the front of the drawers. The room smelled of fresh paint and new baby clothes as I filled the drawers with cloth diapers and tiny pajamas. I suddenly went completely still, and I gasped. *I never saw Jenny in the morning.* I sat on the floor and figured out the timeline in my head. During the week, I dropped Jenny off at Fern's at 7:25 and didn't pick her up until about 4:40. On Saturday and Sunday mornings, I didn't get home until 6:00 a.m. So, when I got home, I laid Jenny in her crib and didn't get up until 11:00 a.m. *I never saw Jenny's face in the morning light!* I folded my body in agony over myself at the realization.

Allan was working two jobs, and even with our combined income, it would take a long time to get out of debt. I flinched at the thought of telling Allan I didn't want to go back to work after the baby was born.

One evening, Allan was watching TV, and I sat down beside him on the navy sofa. "I need to talk to you." He got up, turned the knob of the TV to the left, and sat back down. I stood up and paced.

"Allan, I never saw Jenny in the morning."

Allan rubbed his forehead and then leaned forward with his elbows resting on his knees. "Yeah—so?"

"I just can't stand the thought of not seeing the baby in the morning." My face turned white, and my lips trembled. "I don't want to work after the baby is born."

Allan went completely still, and his eyes turned dull.

"I know we don't have any money—but I'd rather be poor than not be with my baby."

Allan leaned back on the sofa, sighed, and answered with a small nod.

For a long time after that, Allan didn't talk quite as much.

# CHAPTER THIRTY-SEVEN

On a Saturday morning in March, I sat in our kitchen on one of the two wooden chairs that went under the tiny dinette table. Rays of sunlight streamed through the kitchen window, but it still felt like winter with the outside thermometer reading twenty-three degrees. I wrapped my heavy pink robe as tight as I could around my huge belly, and I leaned over my Bible. By this time, I had read nearly the entire Bible, and we were getting to the end of our Navigator Study on Thursday nights. I closed my Bible, crushed out my cigarette, and took a drink of Coke. With my arms crossed, I settled back in the wooden chair and stared out the window, and my mind started to reel. *Although I had prayed with Eva Mae years ago, and I had listened to Allan pray six months ago, I had never—really—purposefully repented of my sins and given my life to Christ.* When I searched for the answer to the question, "How can I get to heaven?" my motive was to be with Jenny. Going to hell never entered my mind. Now, I understood that

I should also have been asking another question: "I'm headed to hell because of my sin, so how can I get rid of *that*?" So, I unfolded my arms, sat up, laced my fingers together, and rested my hands on top of the dinette table. I closed my eyes and tipped my head downward. At that moment, I repented of my sins and gave my life to Jesus Christ.

◆ ◆ ◆

Every day for almost eight months, Allan and I asked God for a healthy, happy baby. We knew what might happen. On the morning of April 15, I grabbed my prepacked hospital bag and headed to Wesley Medical Center. It was exactly nine months and four days after Allan and I married.

When the blond receptionist saw me waddle through the door, she called for a wheelchair and pointed to the elevator. Allan took my bag and stepped back when a maternity nurse in a white starched uniform seated me in the wheelchair and adjusted the metal feet. Allan lingered behind as she pushed the wheelchair down the hall, and when the elevator door dinged, she turned it around and backed my wheelchair into the elevator. When we reached the maternity floor, she took the bag from Allan and pointed to the waiting room. "I'll come get you after we get her set up in her room."

They led me to my room and handed me a light-blue cotton gown. After I was settled, Allan came in, and we both lit up cigarettes and chatted. After a few hours, the contractions were just right, so the anesthesiologists inserted a catheter tube to deliver pain medicine. "This will help you not feel it," he said.

I jerked my head toward the doctor. "Really?"

He gave me a playful grin. "Oh yeah. You'll get a dose of pain medicine every two hours." Before long, my legs were numb.

When I was in the delivery room, the epidural removed the physical pain, but it didn't remove the agonizing fear as to the health of the baby. As soon as my nine-pound, eight-ounce baby girl was born, the scrub nurse wrapped her in soft white blankets and left the delivery room. Dr. Robinson was waiting. After the delivery room door closed, I bit my lip and avoided eye contact with the other nurses as they put away medical devices, wiped down bed rails, and lifted my numb legs so they could adjust the clean gown they had just slipped over my head.

After they hoisted me onto the bed in my room, I asked the nurse about my baby. She noticed my stiff neck and watery gaze.

"Dr. Robinson is going over her with a fine-tooth comb." She smiled down at me and patted my shoulder before she left the room.

A few minutes later, Dr. Robinson lightly knocked on the door and peeked in. I took deep breaths and wet my lips. A wide grin spread across his face. "She's perfect."

❖ ❖ ❖

A nurse would bring the babies to the mother's room to feed them every four hours, but the first feeding was six hours after the baby was born. In preparation for the baby coming, we had to turn off the TV, not use the phone, put out our cigarettes, and wash our hands.

The white-capped nurse grinned as she leaned over me and placed my dark-haired baby in my arms. Kendra was tightly wrapped in a soft pink blanket. The nurse then handed me a small bottle of formula. Her voice had a warm tone to it. "She probably won't eat much."

I took the bottle and pressed the nipple against her lips. She frowned and twisted her head to the side. "Hey now," I whispered as I adjusted and lightly bounced her. "You can do this." Kendra turned her head back toward the bottle, and I swirled the nipple around her lips. My heart raced when she opened her mouth, wrapped her lips around the nipple—and sucked.

✦ ✦ ✦

After Kendra was born, I couldn't go to the cemetery every day, but all through the winter, when I gazed at the snow and felt the freezing temperatures, my throat constricted at the thought of how cold Jenny must be. I took a small amount of comfort in knowing that we paid extra money for the vault. *That would surely keep her warmer.* Although I couldn't sleep as much now, the deep, dark depression lingered.

One afternoon in May, the temperature was seventy-five degrees, and the sky was blue. I opened the living room windows and the window in the kitchen, and a soft breeze swept through both rooms. I had just washed and dried dishes, set them in kitchen cabinets, dusted furniture, and vacuumed all the floors. I lifted Kendra from the bassinet that sat beside our bed and was strolling through the living room and into the kitchen when I felt it. The feeling was so distinct that I stopped midstride and stood there. The deep heaviness in my heart—the black hole that I lived in—suddenly felt just a tiny bit lighter. I could almost visualize a sliver of light that crept through the darkness that had surrounded my inner being for almost nine months. I felt a fragment of hope that maybe—just maybe—I might be able to live again.

# CHAPTER THIRTY-EIGHT

I sat on one of the metal-legged, gray-padded chairs in the waiting room of Dr. Robinson's office. Kendra lay sleeping in my arms, and another mother crossed her arms and watched her toddler drag toys out of the toy box. Before long, Dr. Robinson's nurse opened the door, called Kendra's name, and showed me into the examination room.

"Just undress her down to her diaper, and Dr. Robinson will be in shortly." She winked, smiled, and closed the door behind her.

Kendra woke up when I took off her shoes and pulled her lacy pink dress over her head. I folded her dress, tucked her socks into her shoes, and stacked them at the end of the examination table. I wrapped her blanket around her and set her on my lap as we waited.

When Dr. Robinson opened the door, his eyes darted between me and the clock on the wall. "Well, now," he said. "How's everything going?" He picked up Kendra and unwrapped her as he set her on the examination table. I leapt to my feet and explained that she had been up half the night crying and running a low-grade fever. He felt her body. "She doesn't seem to have a fever now."

"But she's still congested." My eyebrows drew together, and I rubbed my arms.

Dr. Robinson wrapped the blanket back around Kendra and set her in my arms. Then, he sat on the small black-swivel chair and turned toward me as he rested his forearms on his knees and crisscrossed his fingers together. His eyes bore into mine. "Normal children—uh, I mean children who do not have any type of physical problems—have bodies that heal themselves."

I flinched and my eyes widened. "Really?"

The corners of his mouth turned up. "Sure!" Dr. Robinson stood up and picked up his chart. "When she gets sick, just let her rest and give her plenty of liquids, and—maybe—some Bayer Children's Aspirin." He scribbled on his chart and, again, glanced at the clock. "If she doesn't get better in a few days, *then* give me a call." He gave Kendra a quick pat before he opened the door and left.

◆ ◆ ◆

When Kendra was five months old, I got the call that my pregnancy test came back positive. I could feel my heart beat faster, and I couldn't control the smile on my face. On the other hand, when I told Allan, worry lines spread across his face, his muscles tightened, and his skin flushed.

One afternoon, I tucked Kendra in her crib for her afternoon nap and picked up a laundry basket full of diapers, underwear, and baby clothes. I folded each item one by one making sure each tuck and turn lined up perfectly. Then—it hit me. I stopped folding clothes and sat on the navy sofa with my arms folded across my chest. I'd always known that God took care of Jenny, but I suddenly realized that God also *used* Jenny as a magnet to pull me toward Him! I leaned forward and sat with my elbows on my knees, and my hands on my cheeks as I stared off into nowhere. *I would NEVER have searched for God or gone to church or read the Bible unless I'd had a strong enough reason to do so. God gave me that reason—and He did it because He loved ME.* After several minutes, I rubbed my eyes, stood up, and picked up another white cloth diaper out of the laundry basket.

◆ ◆ ◆

Kendra had just started to walk when I sat on an orange-padded waiting-room chair in my obstetrician's office. My eyes followed her every move as she waddled back and forth across the beige Berber carpet. She would stumble and fall every three or four steps, but when she did, Kendra would look up at the lady sitting behind the glass and laugh. The busy brunette receptionist would glance down and smile back. When she did, Kendra would laugh more. I had forgotten that we'd not only prayed for Kendra to be healthy, but we had also prayed that she would be happy.

The white-uniformed nurse called my name, so I wrapped my fingers around the arms of the chair and pried myself off the padded seat. I grasped Kendra's hand and wobbled back to the examination room. The nurse led me through the door and pointed to the table covered with an ironed white sheet. "You can just hop up, and the doctor will be in shortly." She shared a playful grin with Kendra before she traipsed out the door.

Within minutes, the obstetrician strolled into the room as he simultaneously flipped through papers in his folder. His eyes peered through black-rimmed reading glasses that matched his black hair. He was in his mid-forties, and he was all business.

Without looking up from his folder, he asked, "How are you doing?"

I tried to shift my legs to get some relief. In jest, I said, "This is a really big baby, or I'm having twins—or something." For one reason or another, I had not seen the obstetrician for a couple of months.

He put down his folder and turned to me. "Lay back and let's have a look."

With a grunt, I twisted my heavy body around and lay back on the white sheet. The doctor lifted my maternity blouse and began pushing on this side and that side. He finally settled on one upper area on my right side and wrapped his hands all around. His eyes went to the ceiling in concentration as his hands rubbed over that part of my paunch. "I feel a head here," he said. Then, he moved his hands over my huge midriff down to my lower left side. He settled on another area and, again, wrapped his hands all around. "… and I feel a head here."

I jerked. and my eyes bulged. After a period of silence, my voice shook when I spoke. "Do you—do you mean *twins*?"

His eyes were on his papers as he scribbled notes on them. "I'll send you down for a sonogram to be sure."

◆ ◆ ◆

I placed Kendra in her carrier on the passenger side of the Torino and climbed in on the driver's side. I drove straight to Cessna.

No one could go into Cessna until they passed through the guard shack. Every morning, hundreds of employees marched into the small, gray building, found their time cards, punched in the time of arrival, and returned the card to the holder on the wall. This routine was repeated every afternoon at 4:30. The pudgy, sixty-year-old, balding guard knew everyone by name.

When I trekked into the guard shack, the guard smashed his cigarette into an ashtray that overflowed with cigarette butts. He picked up the black receiver and dialed Allan's extension. Within ten minutes, Allan trotted through the door and spotted me sitting in a folded chair with a cigarette in my hand and yacking with the guard. He pulled up a chair across from me and leaned in with his fingers laced and his forearms resting on his knees. "What's up?"

I couldn't talk, but he could read my face. My whole face glowed, and my smile reached up to eyes that sparkled. After a few moments, he finally spoke. "Twins."

I barely nodded. For a few moments, Allan went completely still. Then, a smile slowly crept over his face. "Well—I guess I can get a third job." We both stood up and wrapped our arms around each other.

# CHAPTER THIRTY-NINE

The morning after the doctor told me I was having twins, I felt contractions. We climbed into the used red Mustang that we had paid cash for out of the money we got off the Torino, and we headed to Wesley Hospital. After a few tests, the doctor sashayed into the room holding a clipboard. "One of the babies is breech." Allan rubbed his chin, and we both stared at the doctor.

"Breech?"

He smiled politely and looked at his notes as he spoke. "That means he's turned upside down, and his butt is coming out first." When he didn't hear a response, he raised his eyes from his clipboard and onto our faces. He stopped writing.

"His head is supposed to come out first, so it's a little risky. You'll have to have a Caesarean section."

◆ ◆ ◆

Kendra was thirteen months old when I had twins. My son, Jeremiah, was born first, and he weighed five pounds, twelve ounces, and my daughter, Renata, weighed five pounds, eleven ounces. The maternity ward sounded of quiet laughter and newborn baby cries mixed with the smell of fresh-cut flowers and disinfectants. Because I'd had a C-section, I couldn't leave the hospital—or see Kendra—for six days. All the nurses in starched white uniforms and white caps wore smiles, but when they saw the dark circles under my eyes, they'd tell me that I needed to get some sleep. I explained that I wasn't going to see my one-year-old daughter for *six days*, but none of them seemed to understand the gravity of the situation. When they rolled the babies out of my room and into the nursery, I immediately sat up in my bed and reached for a cigarette. It was no use even trying to sleep.

Allan found a stairwell that I could access from my floor. The twins were born on a Monday, and it was Friday when I tiptoed down the wax-tiled hallway and crept up to the metal door that opened into the empty stairwell. I pushed against the bar on the door, and Allan stood on the other side holding Kendra in his right arm. She squirmed in her yellow sundress as he held the door open with his left hand, and I stepped onto the cool cement platform. I sat down on the cold metal stairs and put out my hands toward Kendra.

"Hi, there—how are *you*?" I smiled as I wiggled my fingers for her to come. She drew back as if she had never seen me before and clung to Allan. Her bottom lip puckered up, and her chest heaved up and down as her eyes filled with tears. My heart hurt, and I felt numb all over. I reached for her again, but she turned her head away and clung tighter to Allan. We were afraid someone would see us, so I stepped back through the door and snuck back to my room.

Later that day, Dr. Robinson came into my room. "I saw Kendra today, and she cried and wouldn't come to me." I looked at him with anticipation.

"Of course not," he said as he scribbled something on the babies' chart. His voice was light and bubbly. "You disowned her!" Before he scuttled out the door, he looked at me with a smile and eyes that crinkled. He didn't seem to notice my rounded eyes and frozen body—but the nurse did. After he left, she gave me an understanding smile and put her hand on my arm.

"Don't worry. My mom once told me that I disowned *her* when my little sister was born."

"Really?" I raised my eyebrows and gave her a questioning gaze. "What happened?"

"Oh—we're fine now." She chuckled. "In fact, we're really close."

The tension I felt inside started to diminish, and I felt light—even hopeful.

✦ ✦ ✦

Two years later, we were settled into a white house with black shutters and a one-car garage. Our house had green shag carpet, three bedrooms, one bathroom, and a full basement with wall-to-wall yellow and orange Berber carpet and dark-wood paneling. Toys and playthings lined the walls. Allan made the money, and it was my job to make sure we could live on it.

I had read every word of Proverbs 31 and followed it as best I could. At 5:30 a.m., I'd reach over to the clock on the bedside table and push down the button on top. I'd wash my face, brush my teeth, smear foundation over my face, spread eyeliner across my eyelids, rub lipstick on my lips, and unroll my hair. Allan was up at 6:00, and he didn't eat breakfast, so I'd comb my hair, make the bed, and straighten up while he took a bath, dressed, and left.

By 6:30, I either pulled bacon and eggs out of the refrigerator, or I'd take flour and baking powder out of the kitchen cabinets for pancakes. At 7:00 each weekday morning, my three kids sat at the kitchen table in front of either bacon and eggs, pancakes, or oatmeal. Most of the time, they'd pick at their food, but I wouldn't wipe off their hands and faces until they'd eaten *everything*—no matter how long they had to sit there.

After I took frozen meat from the freezer for that night's meal, we all traipsed back to their bedrooms. I threw open their closet door and pulled out play clothes, which I had painstakingly sewn, and shoved them over their brown hair and helped them push their arms through armholes. Then, I'd comb Jeremy's hair to the side, and I dipped the comb in water to slick back the hair of Kendra and Renata before I wrapped their ponytails with a rubber band and tied a bow with a ribbon that matched their clothes. At 8:00, they were in the basement playing and fighting.

At 8:01, I reached the top of the refrigerator, turned the dial of the radio to the right, and listened to John MacArthur then Chuck Swindoll then R. C. Sproul while I worked on the chores that I had assigned myself for that particular day: Mondays I did laundry, Tuesdays—cleaning,

Wednesdays—baking, Thursdays—laundry (again), and on Fridays I went to the grocery store. Nearly *every* day, though, I had to spend some time bending over the sewing machine making clothes from material that cost a dollar a yard and cut from a pattern that offered a variety of styles for some sort of clothing. I could make a play outfit—or a dress—or a shirt for about one dollar each!

On Fridays, I'd wheel two grocery carts through Dillons. I pushed one cart in front of me filled with groceries, and I pulled the other cart behind me filled with kids. Halfway through the store, I'd hand each of them a donut, which kept them happy and quiet for the rest of the shopping trip. For each item I put in the cart, I'd check it off my list and write the price beside it. I couldn't go over my $50.00 weekly budget, which included groceries—and everything else I needed for the house. Since it was cheaper to make meals from scratch, my cart was filled with things like flour, baking powder, sugar, raw fruit, frozen vegetables, and hamburger meat.

In the evenings, Allan did the dinner dishes while I rotated kids through the tub and washed them from top to bottom. Then, I laid their heads across my lap and scrubbed their teeth as they twisted their heads this way and that. At 7:30, we read their Bible story and knelt with them by each of their beds to pray. After routine kisses and Allan's playtime, we tucked them in, and I marched into the kitchen to pop popcorn and mix up cherry Kool-Aid.

Four nights a week at 8:00, the doorbell rang, and a single guy and a single girl traipsed into our living room with a Bible under their arm and a copy of the Navigator's "Studies in Christian Living" in their hands. Allan and the single guy sat on opposite ends of the navy sofa, and I sat across the kitchen table with the single girl. While we all munched popcorn and drank Kool-Aid, we'd have our guests cite the verse they'd memorized for that week. After that, we'd go over each question in the Navigator booklet.

At 11:00, we'd linger by the front door saying our goodbyes. After we shut the front door, I headed for the bathtub, and Allan crawled into bed. By midnight, I crawled into bed beside him to the sound of his soft snore.

I lay on my back with my fingers crisscrossed and resting on my chest. As usual, I whispered the Lord's Prayer. After that, I'd ask God to "Please tell Jenny hello and that I love her." When I finished, I turned to my side and tucked my arm under my head. I knew Jenny could not come back to me, but I also knew that—someday—I would go to her.

"And they overcame him by the blood of the lamb and by the word of their testimony, and they did not love their lives to the death."

*Revelation 12:11 (NKJV)*

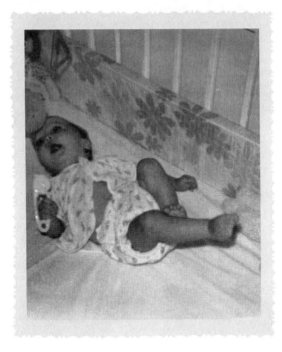

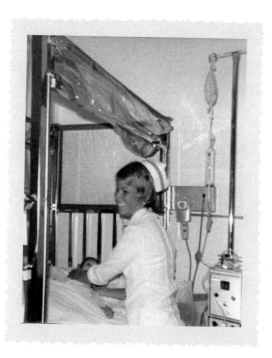

Made in United States
Cleveland, OH
05 May 2025

16672502R00150